Philip Johnson /
Alan Ritchie Architects

Philip Johnson / Alan Ritchie Architects

Introduction by Paul Goldberger

THE MONACELLI PRESS

We wish to thank John Manley, whose continuous efforts
and exemplary design talents have contributed greatly for
over forty-six years to the success of the office.

First published in the United States of America in 2002 by
The Monacelli Press, Inc.
902 Broadway, New York, New York 10010.

Library of Congress Cataloging-in-Publication Data
Philip Johnson/Alan Ritchie architects / introduction by
Paul Goldberger.
p.   cm.
ISBN 1-58093-084-0
1. Philip Johnson, Ritchie & Fiore Architects.
2. Johnson, Philip, 1906– . 3. Architecture—United
States—20th century. 4. Architectural practice,
International. I. Goldberger, Paul.
NA 737.P455 A4   2001
720'.92'2—dc21   2001031202

Printed and bound in Italy

Designed by Abigail Sturges

Contents

Foreword

Alan Ritchie

I have had the privilege and pleasure of working with Philip Johnson for more than a quarter of a century. This monograph chronicles the last decade of our close working relationship.

These ten years have been a period in which we have continued to design and construct the large-scale projects for which the firm has been known throughout the years, projects like New York's majestic Chrysler Center, which has reclad the Kent Building and resulted in the spectacular glass pyramids that echo the distinctive spires of this world-famous building; the residential development at Riverside South, built on a scale not seen in Manhattan for fifty years; and the multifaceted apartment building we are designing on Spring Street in lower Manhattan.

In Fort Worth, we have created a dramatic addition to the Amon Carter Museum—a building Philip Johnson originally designed in 1961. In Boca Raton, our four-acre master plan for First Union Bank is a mixed-use development including a seven-story office tower and a two-story bank building with a landscaped pedestrian plaza and arcade.

Since 1990, we have for the first time taken on a limited number of small-scale projects; these offer us very different design challenges. Among such projects are a Colorado ski house designed as a series of cylinders and carved into a hillside in Telluride; a playful children's museum set on an island in the middle of an artificial lake in Guadalajara, Mexico; and an island vacation house in the Turks and Caicos Islands, which was developed as a cluster of linked pavilions.

During the last decade, we have continued to build our practice by focusing on what we know best with the help and unerring eye of Philip Johnson. As Paul Goldberger notes, ours is a practice focused on reshaping classic architectural form into entirely new and surprising works of architecture. Our continuing fascination with and focus on architecture as an art form, using geometric shapes and sculptural forms, informs our current thinking on the creation of buildings as habitable sculpture.

Introduction

Paul Goldberger

In 1966, in an essay introducing *Philip Johnson: Architecture 1949–1965*, published on the occasion of Johnson's sixtieth birthday, Henry-Russell Hitchcock noted that numerous architects of the twentieth century, including Frank Lloyd Wright, Walter Gropius, and Mies van der Rohe, "have continued productive into their seventies and eighties. So one may hope will Philip Johnson." Hitchcock's hopes have been more than realized, since Johnson has worked not only through his seventies and eighties but into his nineties as well. In collaboration with Alan Ritchie, who has worked with him for over twenty-five years, Elizabeth Murrell, and his long-time associate John Manley, who has worked with him since 1955, Johnson at age ninety-five continues to design actively from an office high up in the Seagram Building, the place that has served as the backdrop for much of his career: he collaborated with Mies van der Rohe in the building's creation, assembling his first large office to build the tower; he was himself the designer of the celebrated Four Seasons restaurant at the base of the building; and he located his office at Seagram during the years his firm was doing its best-known commercial and institutional work, in the 1960s, 1970s, and 1980s. After Johnson and Ritchie established the present firm it seemed natural to return to what has been, for Johnson, a nearly holy address.

Of those architects and artists lucky enough to continue working into their ninth or tenth decades, some, like Frank Lloyd Wright and Pablo Picasso, produce work that has an almost wild intensity to it, as if their creative powers were turned on overdrive. Others, like Mies van der Rohe and Wallace K. Harrison, approach this phase of life more as a gentle coda, their last works a recapitulation rather than a new period. Philip Johnson has never believed much in recapitulation. His defining characteristic as an architect has always been his instinctive ability to sense new directions. Together with Alan Ritchie he continues, in his latest work, to probe them. Sculptural form—or the way in which sculptural form translates into architectural presence—is what has interested Johnson for most of the last decade, and the work the office has produced since Johnson and Ritchie formed their practice involves both new kinds of shapes and new ways of using classic architectural form to make entirely new works of architecture.

Throughout his career Johnson has danced back and forth between his two lifelong passions, for architectural history and for pure form and shape. The two have never really been separate: history has always informed his form-making, and his eye for abstract, sculptural form has always affected his historical interests. It is no accident that his own house, the Glass House in New Canaan, is at least as much a classical temple as an homage to Mies. It was inspired by Mies, but it was never completely Miesian. Johnson made his building symmetrical and set it squarely and solidly on the ground; it is anchored to the earth, not appearing to float above it, as is Mies's Farnsworth

House, its near contemporary. For all its connection to Mies, the Glass House is really a work of classicism brought to the ultimate degree of abstraction.

In many ways Johnson's entire career has been an attempt to reconcile modernism and historicism—to prove, in one way or another, that even the most startling and radical forms possess some grounding in the architecture that has come before, and to demonstrate a visual connection to this architecture. In Johnson's early years of practice, with Mies van der Rohe as his dominant influence, his historicism was subtle and understated, as at the Glass House. Later it would become far more literal, as he sought in the 1960s to express what he perceived as the richness of classicism and then, in the 1980s, to replicate historical form even more directly in a series of skyscrapers beginning with the A.T.&T. (now Sony) Building in New York. It is hard to know in what direction Johnson's eclecticism would have gone had he not, late in the 1980s, become interested in the work of Frank Gehry, but it is clear that Gehry's architecture, at once highly sculptural and brilliantly architectonic, breathed new life into Johnson's sensibility. Johnson's love of pure form—which in the 1980s was most often expressed not through actual shapes but rather in the design of skyscrapers that seemed to want to stand apart from their surroundings (however much they were full of traditional details)—suddenly became unshackled. The eclecticism fell away. For most of the last decade the majority of the buildings Johnson has designed show Gehry's influence to some extent, and some of them, like Da Monsta, the expressionistic gatehouse of 1993 at his New Canaan estate, are quite literally homages to Gehry. Indeed, in a career that has never wanted for formal influences, Gehry has come to play a role in shaping Johnson's aesthetic that is larger than any other architect since Mies.

It is tempting to think of Johnson's career as a progression from a kind of rigid formalism in the manner of the International Style toward expressionism as represented by Gehry: a course from rules to freedom, from severity to sensuousness, from hardness to softness. The reality, of course, is far more complex. If Johnson has always had the younger architect's tendency to seek out heroes (a remarkable quality to retain late in life!), he has also always had the measured perspective of a scholar. His knowledge of history tempers his choices. Thus he could never truly be a Miesian, at least not in the total sense that Mies's Chicago acolytes would never challenge the master; in every project except the Seagram Building, where the need to defer completely to Mies was unquestioned, Johnson produced variations on Miesian themes that, like the Glass House, are Johnsonian at least as much as they are Miesian.

Yet there is a reason Johnson sought out Mies and not, say, Gropius. He saw in Mies not only purity but also richness and sensuousness. His love of sensuousness and his desire to express it in his own work would become more marked as the years went on, but its roots go back to the very beginning of his career. It is paradoxical that Johnson, who may have done more than any other figure to bring the International Style to prominence in the United States (and, along with Hitchcock, named it), never accepted many of its most basic premises. Johnson has always been firmly non-ideological. He has always been an eclectic, from the beginning.

So in many ways Johnson's journey over more than sixty years from Mies to classicism to a wide-ranging eclecticism to Gehryesque expressionism has not been as much of an evolution as it might appear. I say that not only because of the historical irony that the architecture he and Alan Ritchie are now producing bears a striking resemblance to German expressionism, a style that was roughly contemporary to the International Style—as if Johnson's sixty-year career had brought him almost full circle, from one kind of European modernism to another. The more substantial point is that in this long career that appears so characterized by outward change the premises of Johnson's work have remained constant: to indulge in the aesthetic pleasure of pure form, form that is filtered through the most refined, not to say the most ruthlessly skilled, art-historical eye imaginable.

Alan Ritchie, like other collaborators Johnson has had in his career, balances enthusiastic support for Johnson's aesthetic inquiries with practical concerns. He manages the office and oversees the complex process by which buildings actually get built, a process that Johnson has never had much patience for, and he has made it possible for the office to remain fully active even when Johnson is absent. Ritchie, who first joined Johnson's firm in 1969, was part of the design team behind many of Johnson's best-known projects of the 1980s, such as the A.T.&T. Building and the forty-story office tower at 190 South LaSalle Street in Chicago. Since the formation of Philip Johnson/Alan Ritchie Architects, the office has undertaken projects as large as high-rise housing towers for the Riverside South project in New York, a large office center in Berlin, and a skyscraper proposal for La Défense in Paris. They have also produced projects as small as an outdoor clock for the tiny park in front of Lincoln Center in New York and a piece of public art for a plaza at Case Western Reserve University in Cleveland. And while much of the firm's small-scale work—what the two architects call "sculptural and art projects" rather than pure architecture—has been exceptionally successful, such as the spectacular folly made of chain-link fencing recently completed for an estate outside of New York, and the doghouse for Johnson's estate in New Canaan, it is important to note that one of the best designs Johnson and Ritchie's firm has yet produced is for a twenty-seven-story apartment tower for Hudson

Square, in lower Manhattan, underscoring the firm's continued interest in large-scale work that is both practical and aesthetically innovative.

The Hudson Square tower, like so much of the firm's more ambitious recent work, owes a debt to Gehry, in this case to his office complexes in Prague and Dusseldorf. The shape of the tower is sharp and angular, with constant setbacks and angled sections; its massing is almost prismatic, and the form is so varied as it rises that the floor plan changes with almost every level. Philip Johnson/Alan Ritchie Architects plans to sheathe different sections with different materials, so that the whole appears not as a single mass but as an amalgam of parts, and each section will have a slightly different window detail, although all of the windows will be double-hung, punched out from the solid surface as at Dusseldorf. The building rises from a base that is connected in both scale and detail to the older buildings of the neighborhood.

The tower is thus both contextual and anti-contextual; it connects closely, more closely than most of Johnson's previous work, to its surroundings, but it bursts forth from them, changing significantly as it rises. If this design shatters the traditional dichotomy between buildings that are contextual and those that are not, it breaks away just as decisively from the common categories of modern and historicist in the way in which it employs traditional elements and details as part of a highly sculptural and abstract form. It is at once a collage and a piece of abstract sculpture, and it is not surprising to see that the earliest studies for the project explore the notion of pieces of John Chamberlain's sculpture as an urban tower.

This building holds forth the promise of being one of the most important residential designs in Manhattan, not to mention being one of the finest late works Johnson has produced. Here his sculptural instincts seem to have found a kind of harmonic balance with the energy of the Manhattan skyline—a situation quite different from that in Berlin a few years earlier, where the civic authorities required such compromises in the design of the American Business Center that the result was neither a strong abstraction nor a strong traditional building. (How much more appealing was an early study for this project, which was a version of Da Monsta at New Canaan blown up to civic scale.)

A comrade to the unbuilt design for Berlin, but considerably more buildable, is the Cathedral of Hope in Dallas, a 2,200-seat house of worship that seems at once mountainous and crystalline, a white, prismatic mass that bears a distant relationship to Johnson's Crystal Cathedral in Garden Grove, California, of 1980. But where the Crystal Cathedral was of glass, the Cathedral of Hope will be solid and opaque, less a shimmering tent than a monumental and inward-facing Monsta. A bell tower in the form of a monumental wall has already been finished, and one can only look forward to the completion of the entire project. Not at all uncertain, and indeed now moving rapidly toward completion, is Philip Johnson and Alan Ritchie's addition to one of Johnson's best-known early museums, the Amon Carter in Fort Worth, of 1961. It is more restrained than most of the firm's new work, since it retains the essential part of the original building, which overlooks Fort Worth as from a great propylaeum, and turns it into a lyrical portico for the larger, more understated structure that rises behind it.

Also in Texas is a design of considerable power, and one that stands more or less alone in the firm's oeuvre: the proposal for the architecture school at Texas A&M in College Station. Philip Johnson/Alan Ritchie Architects has proposed a building that has none of the free-form, nonrational geometries of the more expressionistic projects—but it is every bit as inventive. The main section consists of a large, solid wedge, roughly eight stories high, which contains the studios, classrooms, and offices; a trapezoidal plane of glass and steel is set atop it, supported by columns and covering an outdoor plaza. It is a project that has none of the alluring softness of the expressionist work; it may yield interior spaces that are even more startling.

If the late 1990s have not brought any completed skyscrapers as notable as the proposed tower for Hudson Square, it is not for want of ambitious designs. Two proposals for La Défense, in Paris, look, like so much of the firm's work, simultaneously backward and ahead: one is influenced by Mies's famous early skyscraper schemes, another is a soft composition of curving arcs in plan; either one could have been among the more notable essays in late-modernist form-making. And it would not be appropriate to discuss skyscrapers without taking note of the studies the firm produced in 1997 for Times Square, which prefigured the collagelike towers that are now being built there by other architects.

The office of Philip Johnson and Alan Ritchie has continued to accept residential commissions as well as civic and commercial projects, and three large houses now in the final stages of design offer particular insight into the firm's design priorities: a huge house built around a courtyard on a suburban site outside of New York; a house made up of several variations on Johnson's Monsta, gathered together into a cluster on a large site in Israel; and a house for a Caribbean island consisting of sixteen small structures that are abstracted versions of the Pantheon in Rome. In all three cases Johnson is experimenting with the idea of breaking down a large house into component parts, expressing each one as a somewhat different structure, and he is exploring the way in which perception of a single shape is changed when that shape is varied and changed and all the variations are put together to make a single composition.

The suburban house is to be built on a conventional site in New Jersey for a client who admired the Glass House and wanted something similar, but with privacy. Johnson, faced with the dilemma of satisfying his client while not moving backward in his own work, decided to have the living spaces face inward to a private garden that would function as an enclosed courtyard and sculpture garden. The perimeter wall encloses a rectangle 150 by 140 feet, with the long sides parallel to the street; the narrow sides are actually formed by sections of the house, which face each other across the landscaped space. The main living spaces and the master bedroom suite are under a long, high gable on the southeast, Johnson's abstract allusion to the Tudor houses of the neighborhood, while the northwest side of the courtyard is filled with four attached, two-story guest houses for the owner's children and other guests. The long wall closest to the street is actually an enclosed, book-lined corridor connecting the guest wing with the main house.

The house in Israel was designed for an international businessman and art collector who is based in New York and who has known and admired Johnson for years, but has never before been his client. He had seen Johnson's Monsta when it was first added to the Glass House property, and he reacted with pleasure when Johnson suggested that the best way to design the large residential compound the client had in mind would be to make it a kind of gathering of Monsta-like shapes. The shapes are somewhat varied, with larger ones for public rooms and smaller ones for bedrooms. From above, the overall plan of the house looks like an enormous, distorted sunflower, with petals pointing outward from a huge, ovoid center.

The arrangement of Pantheons in the Caribbean is more random, like a tiny village. As with the house in Israel, the different versions of the thematic shape vary considerably in size, with the largest, the living room, forty feet in diameter. The smallest guest room is fifteen feet in diameter; the master bedroom is twenty-eight feet across. Some of the Pantheons are joined together, somewhat like dumbbells, and there are rectangular doors and windows projected from the sides. Overall, the house does not so much replicate the Pantheon as turn it into a kind of building block, making it a multiple and therefore entirely different in meaning: classicism's unique temple becomes an element to be replicated. The house stands as a remarkable late addition to the extraordinary collection of residential designs by Johnson, which actually began slightly before the Glass House, and which has continued for nearly six decades. As at the Glass House, the Caribbean house merges modernism and classicism in a way that is entirely Johnson's own. It marries the power of pure form to the power of connoisseurship, two things that are so deeply intertwined in Johnson's architecture that it is impossible to tell where one leaves off and the other begins.

St. Basil Chapel
at the University of St. Thomas

Houston, Texas

1991

Philip Johnson designed the campus for the
University of St. Thomas in 1957 in a Miesian
vocabulary with a rigorous materials palette of
glass and steel. The new St. Basil Chapel is
integrated into a two-story gallery connecting the
campus buildings. The structure is a white stucco
cube sliced at an oblique angle by a black granite
wall; the granite wall passes through the galleries
on either side and is perforated by doorways,
windows, and an opening holding the church
bells. The entry wall warps outward, like a tent
flap. The interior features a dramatic play
of daylight from hidden sources: an angled
cruciform window, a slot through the dome,
an angled skylight over the altar, and a skylight
over the statue of the Virgin Mary.

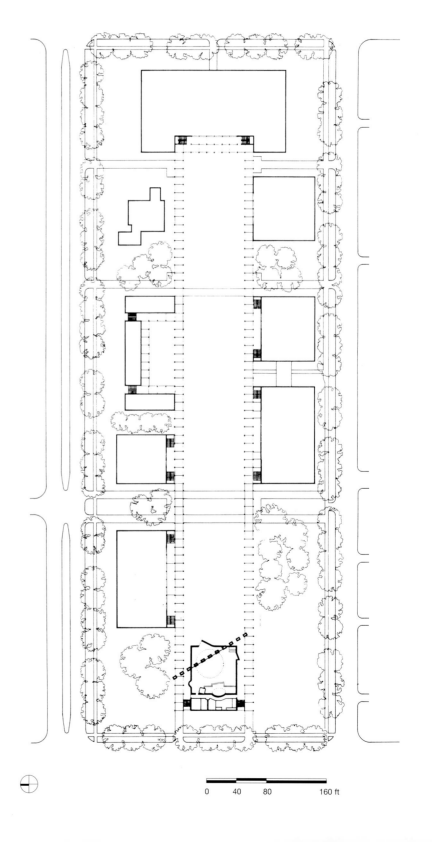

0   40   80   160 ft

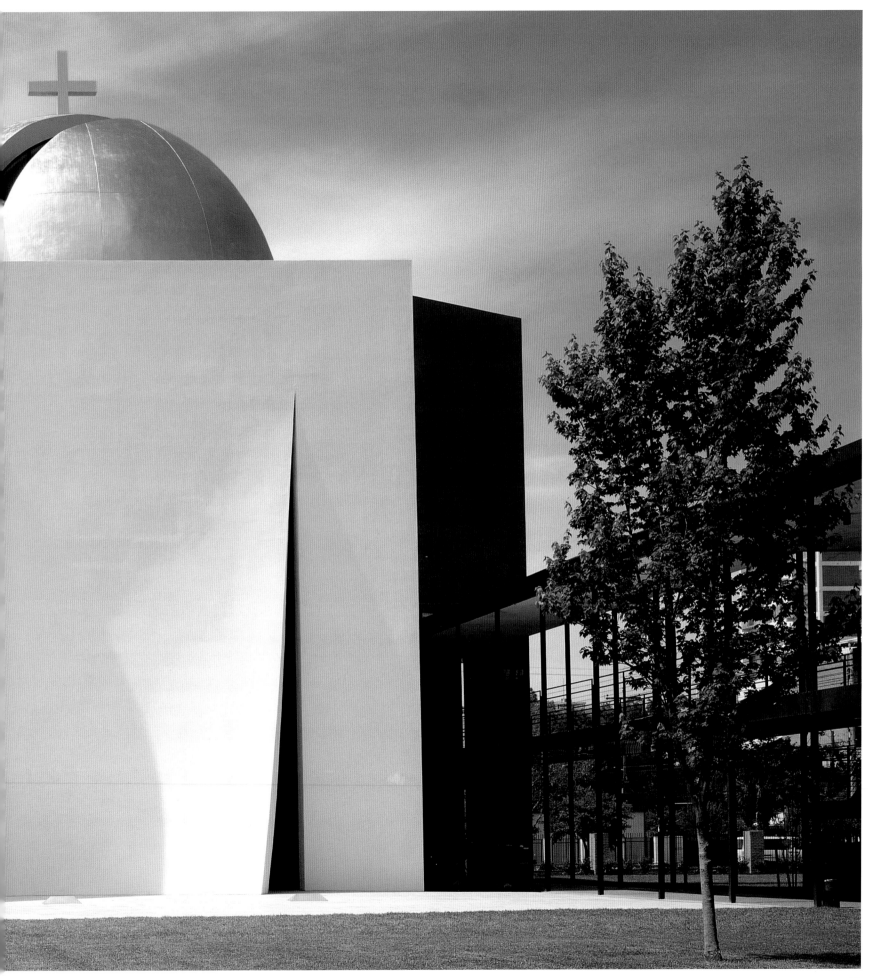

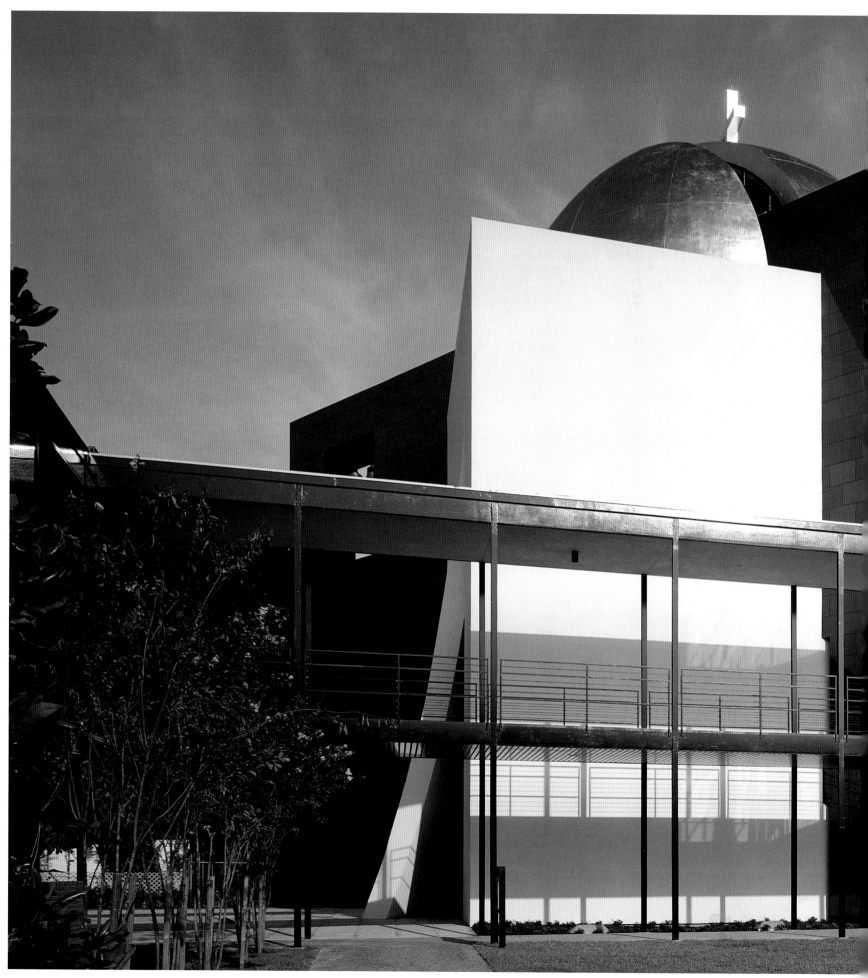

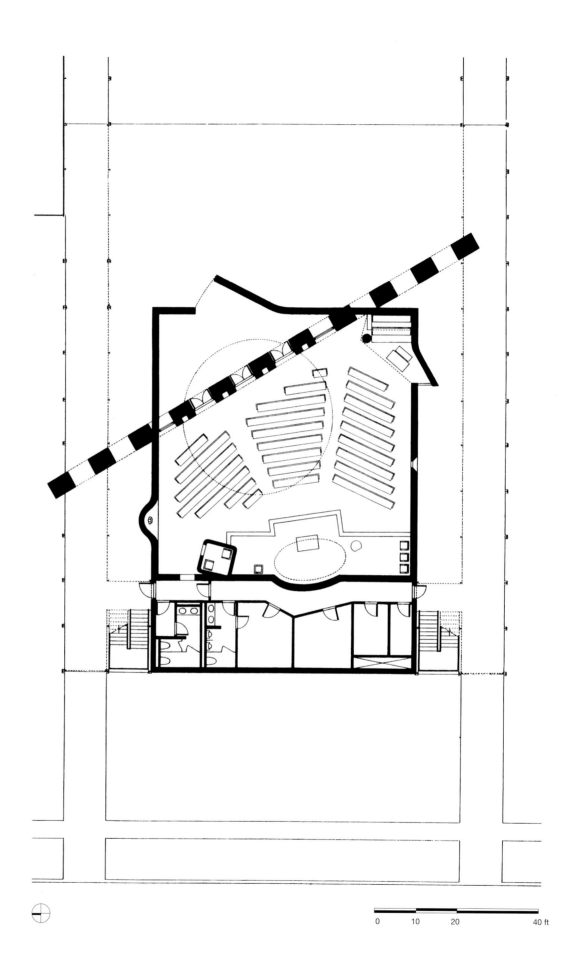

0 10 20 40 ft

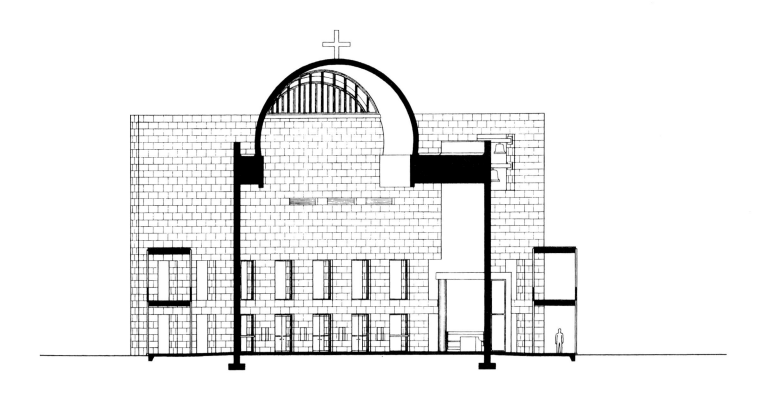

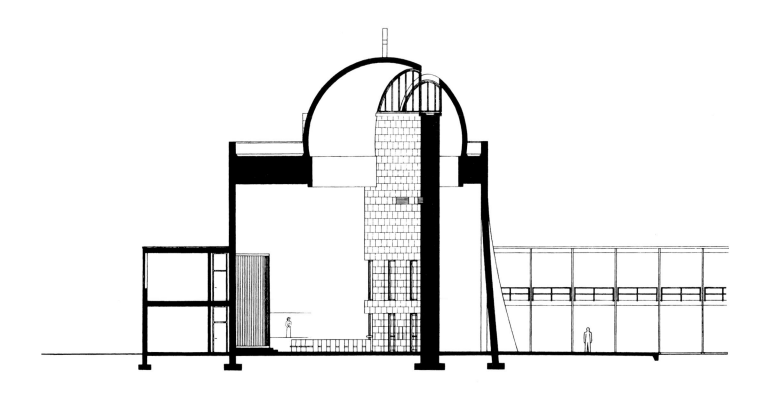

Millennia Walk in Pontiac Marina

Singapore

1992

Millennia Walk is a retail mall in the Pontiac
Marina section of Singapore's business district.
A skylit galleria flanked by shops links a group of
buildings. This galleria is covered by a series of
truncated-pyramid-shaped roof structures clad
on the exterior with lead-coated copper scales.

At the center of the galleria is the great court,
a red-granite-clad room ninety feet in height.
A green metal column-and-beam grid articulates
the walls of the court. Light enters through a large
skylight and smaller clerestory windows with
gold-leafed jambs.

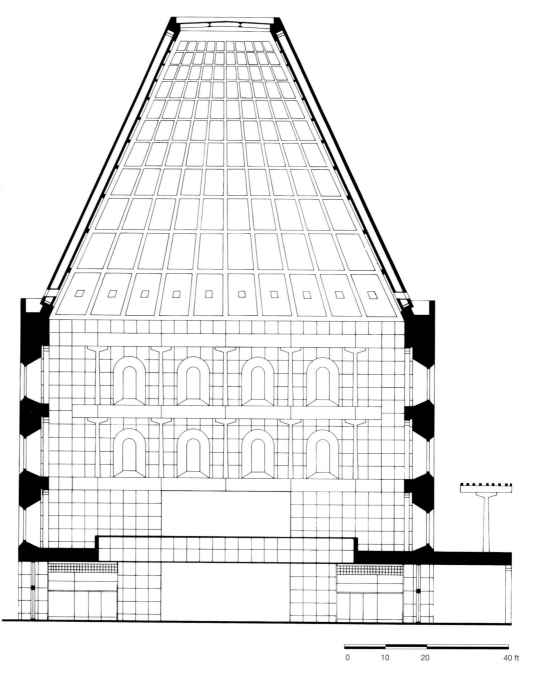

0   10   20   40 ft

American Business Center at
Checkpoint Charlie

Berlin, Germany
1992

Near the former Checkpoint Charlie, this office
building is part of a larger development in Berlin's
rapidly changing urban fabric. To a certain extent,
regulations and context have determined the
building's form: a required stone cornice at a
height of seventy feet; a facade that follows the
curve of the streetfront. Yet these devices are
used primarily to set up a masonry "frame"
or grid that contains the glass volumes of
the building itself. These volumes slip out of
the frame and angle outward at the entries.

The lobby, measured by a grid that determines
the skylight, window, and floor pattern, is an
essay in rationalism. Volumetric elements are
frameless, whereas surface elements are
emphasized with frames. In a gesture derived
from the Italian rationalist Piacentini, the granite
walls stop short of the room's full height and are
transformed into glazed partitions; no cornice
marks this crisp transition.

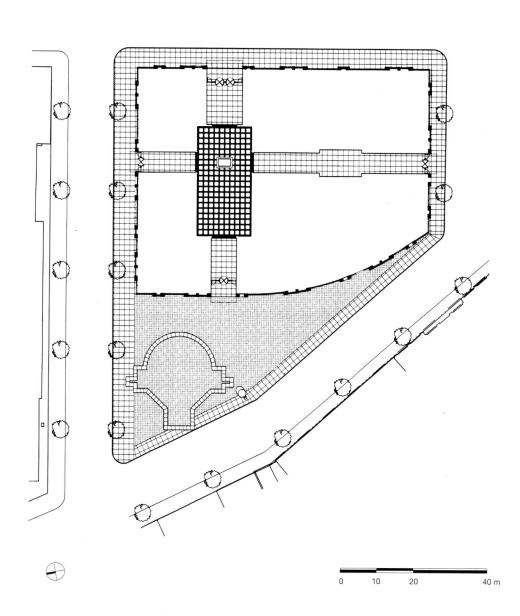

0   10   20   40 m

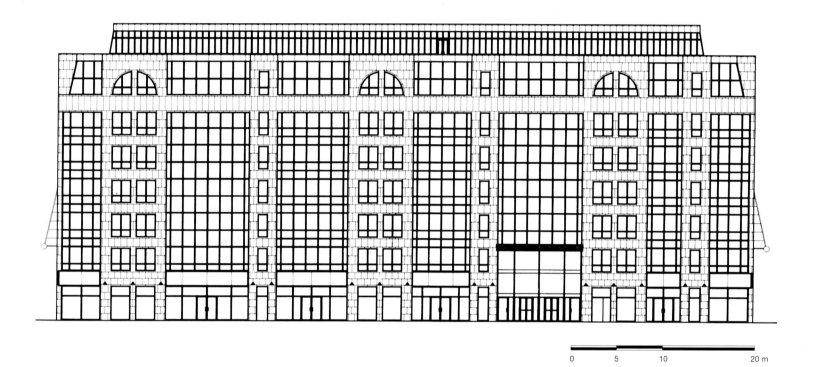

0   5   10   20 m

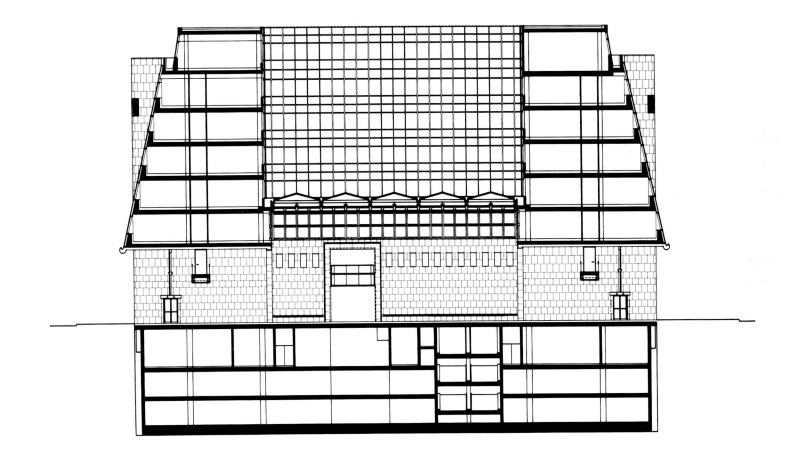

Berlin Fantasy

Berlin, Germany

1992

This project, designed by Philip Johnson, was first presented in Berlin as an exploration of the site of the American Business Center, a critique that was hoped would stimulate debate of the city's outdated zoning regulations. It thus flaunts a freedom of form impossible to achieve within the current guidelines governing cornices, streetfront facades, and zoning envelopes. The project is an inquiry into architectural form in its own right, an elaboration of themes similar to those stated in the Visitors' Pavilion at the Glass House. The non-rational geometry presented is also an essay on the German expressionist architecture that was shaped by such twentieth-century Berliners as Mendelsohn, Taut, Finsterlin, and Mies.

Greater Shanghai Shopping Center

Shanghai, China
Design Competition
1993

Offices, luxury apartments, stores, fountains,
and trees inhabit an urban plaza on busy Nanjing
Road in downtown Shanghai. The Alan Ritchie
design organizes the buildings around a public
square. A thirty-story office and luxury residential
tower is placed on axis with the entry. A six-
story business center is to the east of the square.
At the south and west lie department stores
and a health spa. Fronting on Nanjing Road is
a three-story retail and office building topped
by a roof garden.

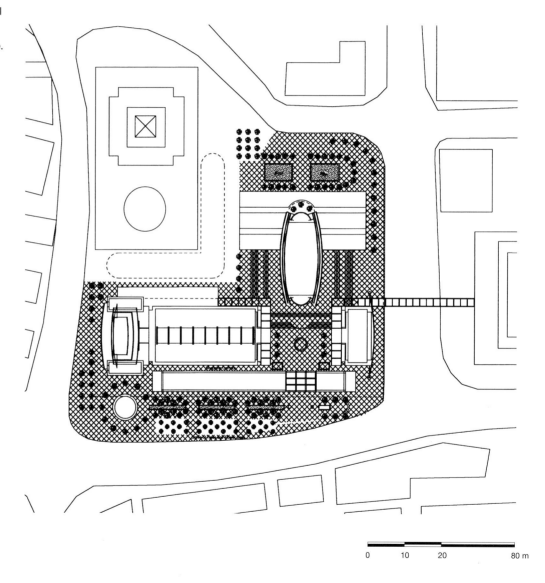

0   10   20   80 m

Borden Hall,
Manhattan School of Music

New York, New York

1993

The Manhattan School of Music is a jazz and classical conservatory, a significant part of New York's cultural life. Shreve, Lamb & Harmon, the architects of the Empire State Building, designed the school in 1932. Alan Ritchie's restoration project returned Borden Hall, the school's principal concert hall, to its previous glory, controlling the tonal elements and lighting to bring out the Art Deco palette of the original.

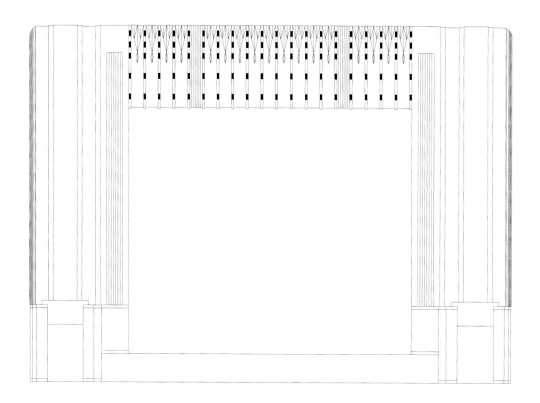

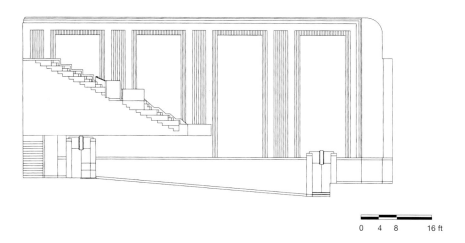

0   4   8   16 ft

Visitor's Pavilion (Da Monsta), Glass House

New Canaan, Connecticut
1993

Philip Johnson has bequeathed his New Canaan estate to the National Trust, which will eventually open it to the public. In anticipation of that event, Johnson designed and built the Visitor's Pavilion, Da Monsta. It is the most recent addition to the landscape that Johnson has developed in New Canaan since 1946, beginning with the Glass House in 1949 and continuing for over half a century, with the property growing from five to forty acres.

Located just inside the entry to the property, the pavilion, a sculpted shelter painted bright red and black, will be a reception and briefing area, a visitor's first stop. An adjoining space is a viewing room for videos about the estate and Johnson's career, narrated by the architect.

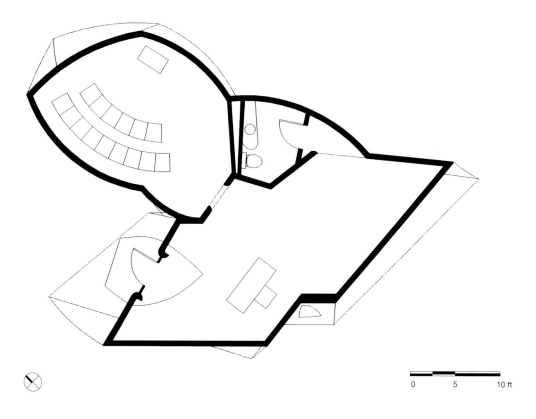

0   5   10 ft

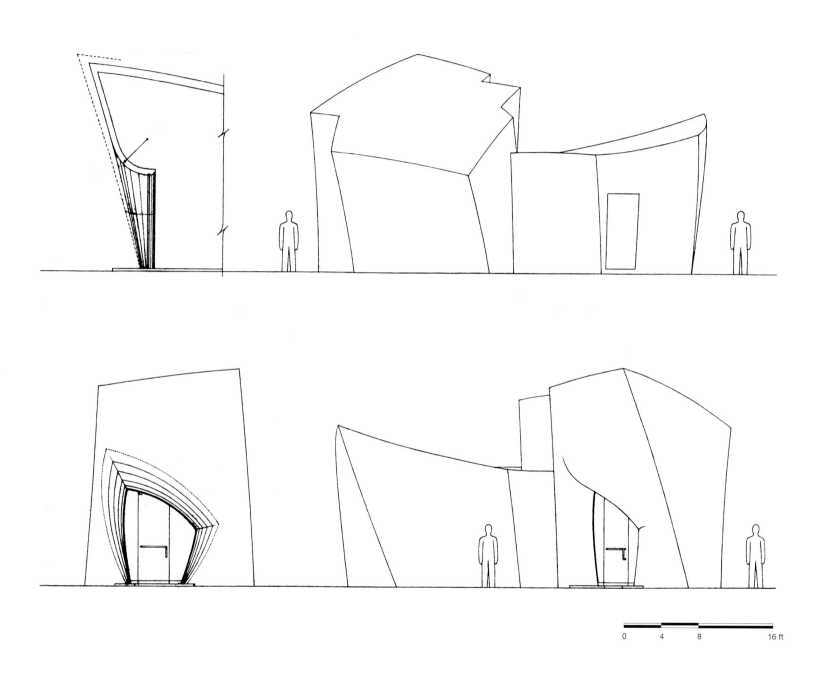

0   4   8   16 ft

Berlin Glockenturm

Berlin, Germany
1994

This clock tower marks the plaza in front of the
American Business Center and also replaces
a 1736 bell from a church previously on the site
but destroyed during World War II. The structure
is a bronze-clad helix ten meters high. It leans
slightly toward the side supporting the church
bell, allowing the bell to hang free and be seen
from down the curving street.

Riverside South Residential Towers

New York, New York
1994

These four towers designed by Philip Johnson and Alan Ritchie are part of a ten-block-long development in New York City on the site of an abandoned railway yard along the Hudson River. Developed by Donald Trump, the site presented an opportunity for a residential development on a scale not seen in Manhattan for half a century. The subject of a decade-long planning process with input from city and state agencies as well as neighborhood planning groups, the design guidelines provided by the Riverside South Planning Commission addressed concerns well beyond the scope of conventional zoning, dictating issues of architectural expression such as window openings, entrances, materials, and detailing.

The towers are primarily residential; they vary in massing while using the same materials, in accordance with the design guidelines. The bases and lower levels—visually separated from the towers as required by the zoning— provide retail space, professional office space, a health club, pool, and parking garage.

National Museum of Korea

Seoul, Korea
Design Competition
1994

The firm's competition entry for the National Museum of Korea groups large ovoid structures together in a plan that is both free-form and also reminiscent of Kahn's rigorous capital complex at Dacca. The approach to the building is via a vast, monumental staircase scaled to the landscape. The building's forms gain their monumentality through severe surface articulation; windows appear only near the top of the spaces. Visitors pass through the grand open courtyard and enter the central exhibit hall; this hall allows access to each of the ovoid structures, which house art and archaeological exhibits.

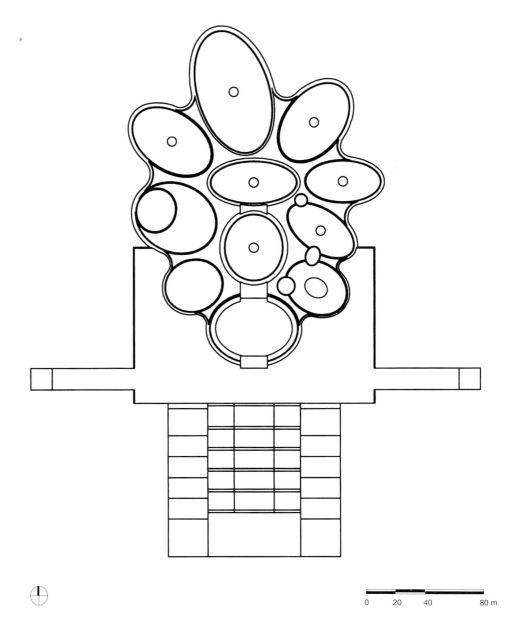

0   20   40   80 m

Sugar Foods Corporate Offices

New York, New York
1994

Sugar Foods Corporation, the maker of Sweet'n Low, relocated its corporate headquarters from lower Manhattan to midtown. The new space, approximately ten thousand square feet, contains offices for chief executives, conference rooms, and support areas. The project included programming, space analysis, interior design and construction, and furniture selection.

Individual offices are placed at the perimeter, giving every office a view. The offices have a simple, contemporary look suited to displaying the art and artifacts collected by the company's chairman. The offices were expanded again in 1996.

New Art Center at Century Center

South Bend, Indiana
1995

Century Center is a civic and cultural complex originally designed by Philip Johnson and John Burgee in 1979. Located in South Bend, the center contains convention facilities, a museum, theater, and recital hall. Each function is contained within its own structure and connected to the others by skylight-covered "streets."

The addition includes a new entry, coffee shop, meeting rooms, and galleries for the art museum's permanent collection. An underground tunnel connects the center to the Collegiate Football Hall of Fame, and a skywalk bridge leads to the Marriott Hotel. New bay windows on the northeast facade overlook the St. Joseph River.

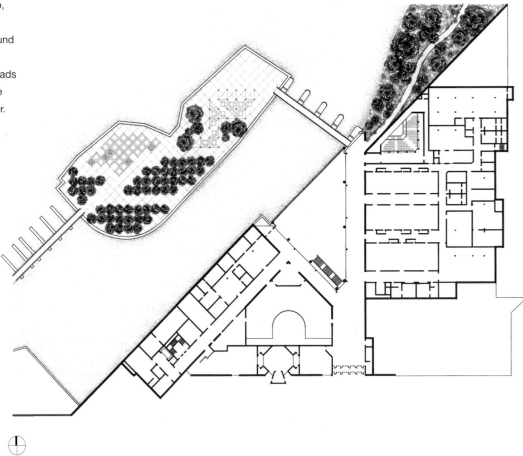

Cathedral of Hope

Dallas, Texas

1995

In 1995 the Dallas branch of the Universal Fellowship of Metropolitan Community Churches, the nation's largest gay and lesbian religious denomination, commissioned a design for a cathedral to house its thousands of worshippers. The resulting massive, free-form structure seats 2,200 and is taller than Notre Dame.

Natural light enhances the cathedral's powerful, solid form. A skylight is poised directly over the altar, at the cathedral's highest point. A beam of light shines down from the aperture like a thick spotlight, the brightest in the church. Another skylight illuminates a sculpture niche. Light also flows in horizontally through the large glass doors at the entry. Uplights and shadows articulate the crystalline planes of the warped walls.

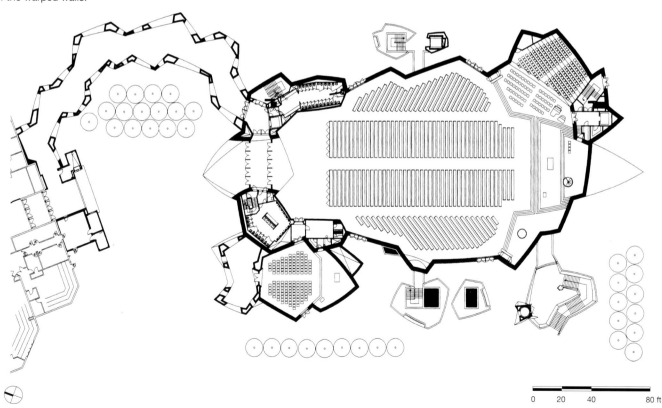

0   20   40   80 ft

Celebration Town Hall

Celebration, Florida

1995

In the mid-1990s, the Disney Development Company built Celebration, USA, a planned community on central Florida wetlands ten miles from Disney World. Disney invited a select group of architects to design the civic, ecclesiastic, and commercial buildings: Michael Graves designed the post office, Robert Venturi and Denise Scott Brown the bank, Cesar Pelli the cinema, Charles Moore the visitor's center.

The town hall, the small community's municipal building, contains an assembly room, civic offices, and an activity center for the local neighborhood association. The brick-clad body of the building sits unassertively within a colonnade of slender columns and a low-pitched roof. The columns are square, straight, narrow, and wooden, derived from the straightforward construction of Caribbean structures and echoing Asplund's woodland chapel.

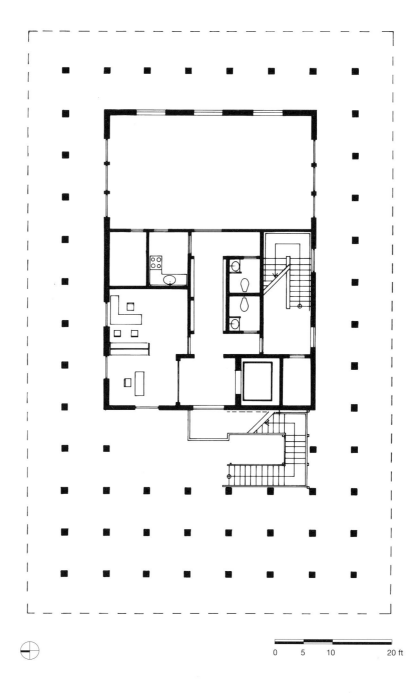

0 5 10 20 ft

Trump International Hotel and Tower

New York, New York
1995

The former Gulf + Western office tower occupies an important site on the corner of New York City's Central Park, adjacent to Columbus Circle. The project involved converting the office building into a hotel and apartment tower. Internally, the conversion required extensive reinforcement of the building's structural rigidity, since tolerance to a building's wind sway is much higher in an office building than in an apartment. Furthermore, the construction of nearby taller buildings along Broadway had created extreme wind-tunnel effects that had not existed when the building was originally erected.

The entire exterior was reclad in bronze-tinted glass. Thin stainless-steel trim elements highlight the vertical lines and projections of the building. The plaza around the building was also rebuilt, requiring a new entry to the subway station at Columbus Circle.

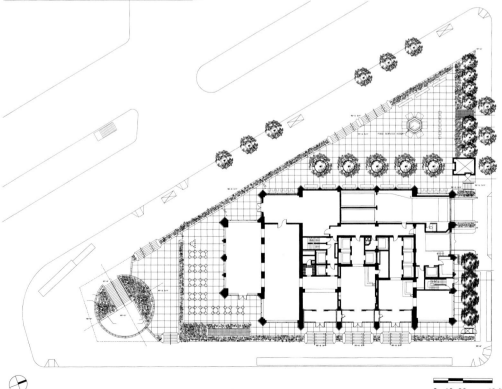

0 10 20   40 ft

Ville de Tremblay

Paris, France

1995

This apartment building, near Charles de Gaulle
Airport, is part of a larger development in the
village of Tremblay, France, designed by a team
of international architects. The building, designed
by Philip Johnson, houses seven apartments
with retail on the ground floor and underground
parking and mechanical. The design adapts the
materials of the immediate context—terra cotta
and stucco—while using them in original ways,
such as roof tile for wall cladding. A conventional
standard-sash corner window is rotated in plan
to allow views of the village green.

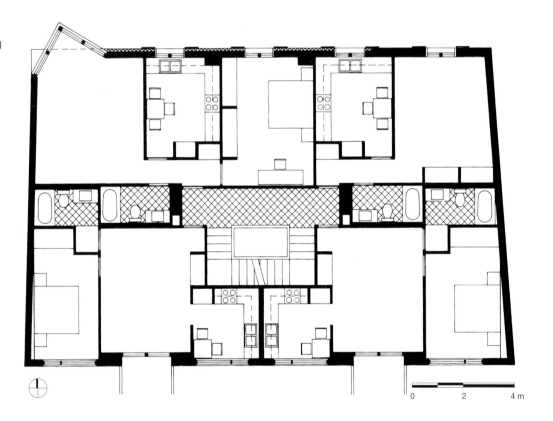

Turning Point at Case Western Reserve University

Cleveland, Ohio

1996

Turning Point is an architectural monument consisting of five sculptural shapes organized around the turning point of a campus pedestrian path. The otherworldly forms are constructed in polyester resin and fiberglass over structural wood veneers. They are approximately twenty feet in height and range from three to seventeen feet in width. The forms converge and diverge around an elusive focal point to create a marker, locus, and monument for the campus.

TimeSculpture at Lincoln Center

New York, New York

1996

This clock sculpture, commissioned by Lincoln Center through a gift from Yaffe and Gedalio Grinberg, sits in Dante Park across from Philip Johnson's 1964 Lincoln Center Plaza and New York State Theater. The triangular design responds to the three primary angles of viewing. The largest clock faces the fountain of Lincoln Center Plaza. Another large clock faces traffic to the north, where Columbus Avenue and Broadway converge. A third faces the traffic on Sixty-third Street as it turns toward Lincoln Center. The fourth and smallest faces an adjacent bus shelter. The sculpture's granite base, three feet six inches high, matches that of Lincoln Center Plaza as well as the base of the statue of Dante with which it shares the park.

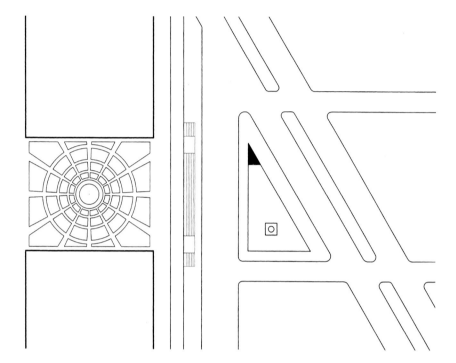

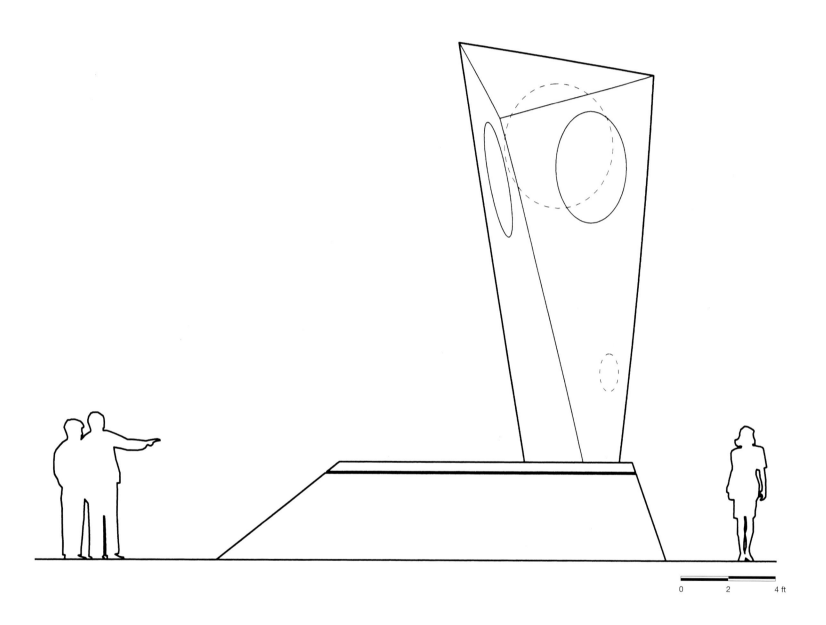

McKinley Center Master Plan

Manila, Philippines
1996

This master plan designed by Alan Ritchie is for
an extensive mixed-use development for the new
Fort Bonifacio district of Manila, just one of the
zones to be developed in the Fort Bonifacio area.
The land is close to Ninoy Aquino International
Airport, about two kilometers from Makati.

Covering sixty-four hectares, the program
describes a small city, including residential
towers, offices, hotels, educational facilities,
a theme park, country club, retail mall, and
chapel. There will also be an eighteen-hole golf
course designed by Arnold Palmer; a light-rail
system will wind its way through the complex.

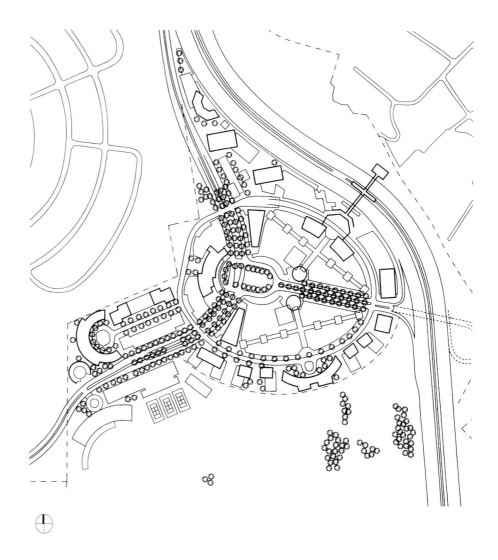

Abu Dhabi Investment Authority Headquarters

Abu Dhabi, U.A.E.
Design Competition
1996

The hexagonal plan and tapering shaft of this tower, conceived by Alan Ritchie, were adapted from Islamic precedents. The layout, which provides many corner and perimeter offices, allows the building to be oriented toward the water and corniche; it is also on axis with the city grid. The tapered shaft creates varied floor sizes.

Deeply recessed windows repeat a pattern of light against shadow to articulate the exterior. Inside, the double-height lobby is red granite, like the facade. The triangles of the coffered ceiling are repeated in the floor pattern. These geometric patterns also have their source in the region's rich history.

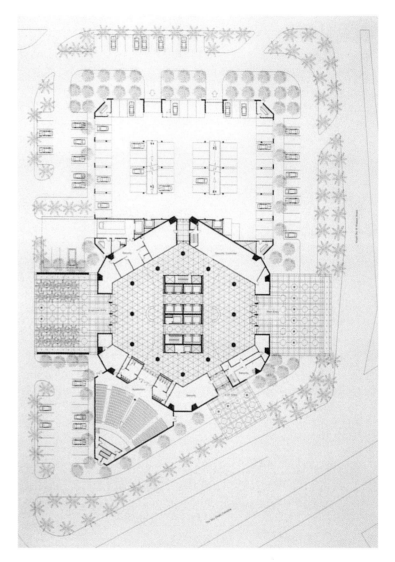

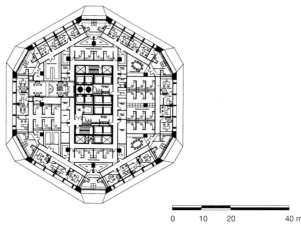

0   10   20   40 m

Amon Carter Museum Expansion

Fort Worth, Texas

1997

At the end of a series of terraces, this addition to Philip Johnson's 1961 design fills the triangular site between Lancaster Avenue and Camp Bowie Boulevard. Providing two floors of public space and three for museum administration and support areas, the addition increases the museum's ability to store, display, and educate the public about its collection of American Western art.

The main entrance, originally through the 1961 pavilion, was relocated to the Lancaster Avenue side of the new brown granite structure. Visitors enter a new double-height atrium, clad in the same Texas shellstone as the original building. A grand staircase leads to the main galleries. The lower galleries, shop, auditorium, and reading rooms are on the ground level. Both floors connect to the original building.

Natural light enters the atrium indirectly through the sides of the great lantern hovering above. The quality and color of the Texas sun—rendered in much of the art on display—make the atrium a place for gathering and an orientation point for visitors throughout the museum.

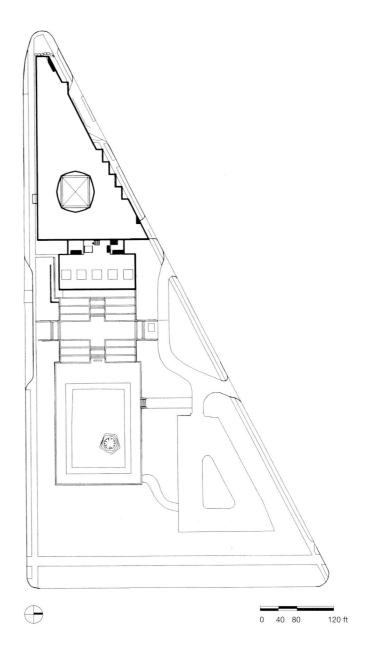

0   40   80   120 ft

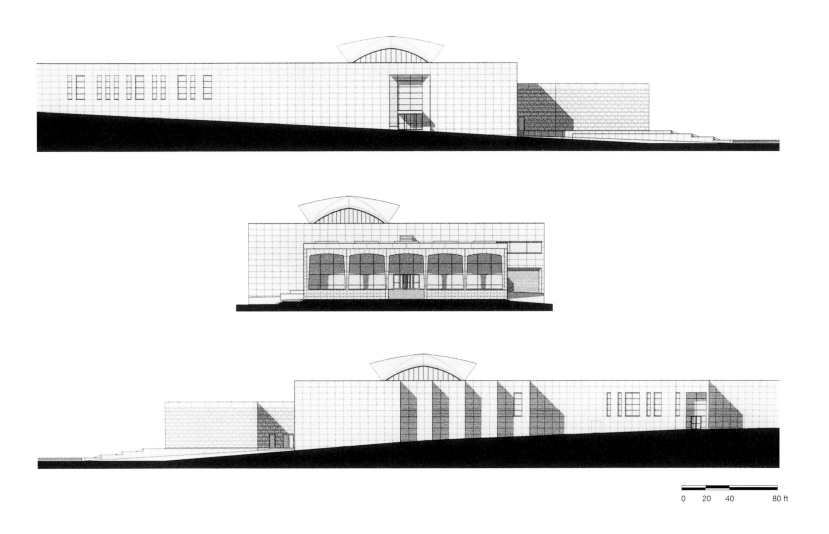

Times Square Site 3

New York, New York

1997

Commissioned by Times Square Center Associates, this project was for one of four parcels at the intersection of Broadway, Seventh Avenue, and Forty-second Street. The design is a high-rise office tower that collides basic geometric forms in conjunction with a bold signage concept; the entire building is thus converted into a graphic collage. The signage concept allows tenants to maintain vision glass but also maximizes the building's commercial value as advertisement or corporate identity. The result transforms the corporate office building exterior wall into a lively artistic display.

Times Square Site 4

New York, New York

1997

The building on Site 4, also commissioned by
Times Square Center Associates, is located
on Forty-second Street and Seventh Avenue
immediately to the south of Site 3. This structure
explores similar massing and graphic concepts,
this time to woo a prospective tenant acclaimed
for cartoon imagery. The simple shapes and
gargantuan graphics exemplify an exuberant
new Times Square focused on the entertainment
industry.

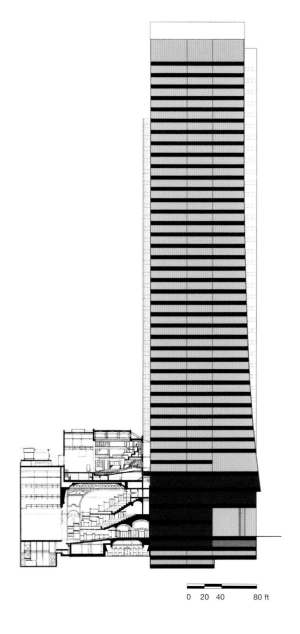

0   20   40   80 ft

Turning Point Park at
Case Western Reserve University

Cleveland, Ohio

1998

Turning Point Park, adjacent to the *Turning Point* sculptures, is an area for students to gather, sit, and study. It is composed of four objects: a fifty-seat amphitheater, a stage-lighting kiosk, a "sit-in" structure, and a "sit-on" structure. The elliptical aubergine amphitheater is held within a swoop of painted aluminum; the seats are formed of bent-wood slats. The muted green stage-lighting kiosk is an inverted cone approximately eighteen feet high with a round windowlike opening. The twenty-one-foot-high powder-blue "sit-in" structure is composed of chain link and painted steel with wooden serpentine benches and tables, while the yellow-painted aluminum, slightly round "sit-on" object is approximately two feet high.

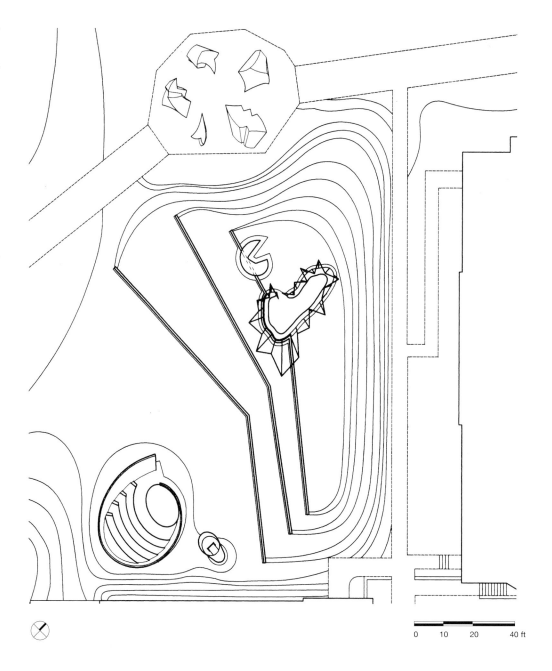

0   10   20   40 ft

Chrysler Center East Tower
Renovation and Expansion

New York, New York
1998

Chrysler Center is a renovation and expansion of the building immediately to the east of the Chrysler Building, the Kent Building, and the walkway between the two. The tower's original brick skin was covered with a gray-green glass curtain wall; a new one-hundred-square-foot bustle was clad in a similar but slightly different green glass curtain wall. The lobby and linking hallways between the buildings were refitted with a variety of materials in a light gray palette.

One of the most striking parts of the refit is a new form on Forty-second Street between the two towers, a space formed by three uplit glass pyramids. Rising seventy feet over the sidewalk, these pyramids provide a unique and unexpected urban marker; the space inside is intended for a restaurant. While the pyramids echo the triangular windows at the top of the Chrysler Building, they are an original and sculptural addition to the streetfront.

333 Westchester Avenue

White Plains, New York
1998

A transformation of the Kraft/General Foods
complex, 333 Westchester Avenue has been
converted into an office park serving White
Plains. The client requested, from a property that
had previously required a uniform appearance,
an identity that reflects a diversity of tenants.
Elliptical pylons now rise over the new entrances
to each of the four quadrants of the building.
The pylons are monuments, silent and abstract
forms that catch sunlight and shadow. Their scale
is that of the complex itself, in order to orient
visitors. The pylons are colored Florida green,
gold, persimmon, and sky blue, and the window
frames of each quadrant have the same color
scheme. The renovation also included lobby
refits; each entrance lobby has its own palette
of maple, ash, eucalyptus, or oak.

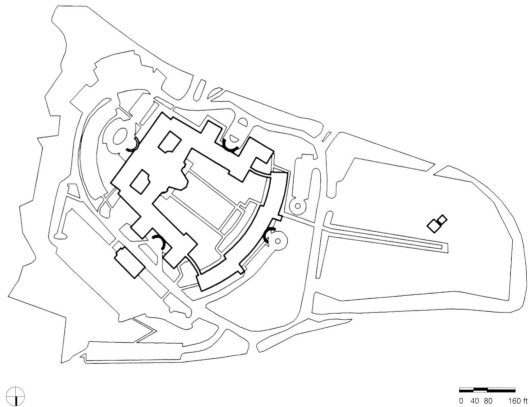

0 40 80   160 ft

First Union Plaza

Boca Raton, Florida

1998

Located in the center of the Boca Raton business district, this four-acre master plan for a mixed-use development includes a seven-story office tower, two-story bank building, and multilevel parking garage. The front faces of the two primary rectangular building masses—the office tower and the bank—are scooped out to unify the forms and create a landscaped pedestrian plaza, now called First Union Plaza, at the corner of Federal Highway and Camino Real. The project is further united by a lively play of complementary stucco colors and textures drawn from the Addison Mizner tradition in local architecture.

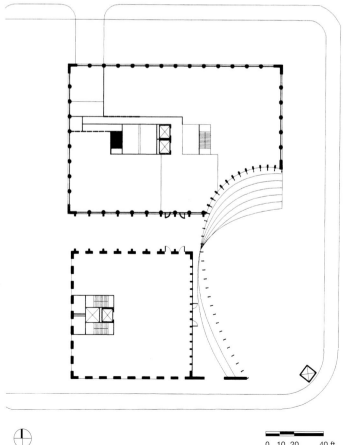

0 10 20   40 ft

Ski House

Telluride, Colorado
1998

This Colorado ski house is made up of three separate facilities: the main house, pool house, and master suite. A footbridge leads to the self-contained master suite, while the structure that houses the lap pool and steam room lies to the southeast. In addition, a hot tub and barbecue pit, carved out of the hill, face the wintertime sun.

Cylinders of varying sizes rise through the main house, like the towers of a fortress. The largest contains a staircase; others are chimneys and storage closets. Walls spring from one cylinder to the next at varying angles, defining the limits of the interior spaces. Living areas in the main house face south, toward an uninterrupted view of the landscape; bedrooms face the creek.

The circular motif established in the plan of the first floor is continued in the windows of the upper stories. Their random sizing and placement contrast with the rectilinear structure of the windows on the floors below.

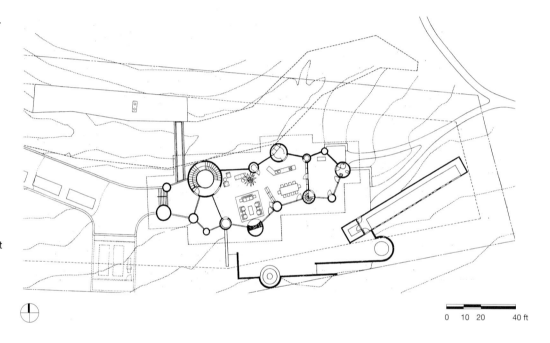

0   10   20   40 ft

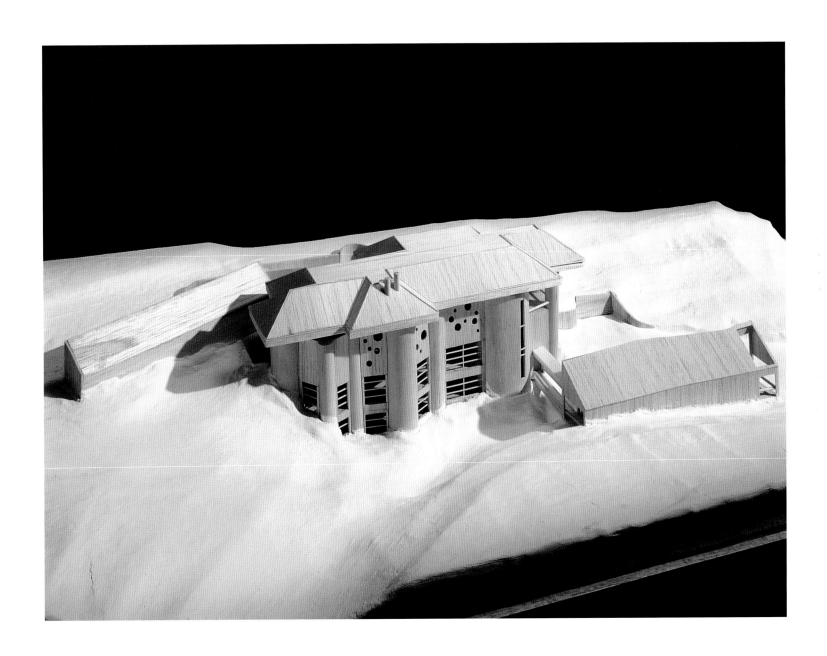

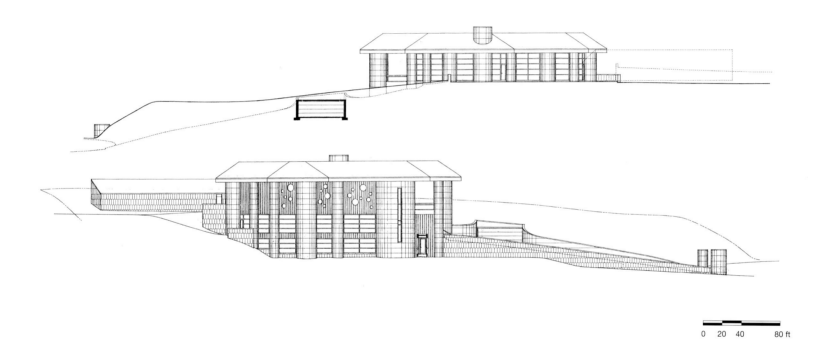

Chain Link Garden Pavilion

North Salem, New York

1999

The geometry of this garden structure in upstate New York is formed as a cluster of intersecting, tilted pyramids. One segment is open to allow entry. The pavilion is fabricated of white chain link connected to a white-painted steel frame. The pavilion's weightless, floating quality is reflected in a nearby pond.

Texas A&M School of Architecture

College Station, Texas

1999

This building for the Texas A&M architectural school is an exercise in contrapuntal design. The main body of the building is shaped like a solid wedge; lifted off this wedge is a trapezoidal plane of glass and steel. This plane is supported by columns at the top and bottom edges and shelters an elevated student plaza in front of the building. The window patterns vary from ribbon windows on the back facade to randomly scattered small windows on the other facades. An elevator tower pins the elements together vertically.

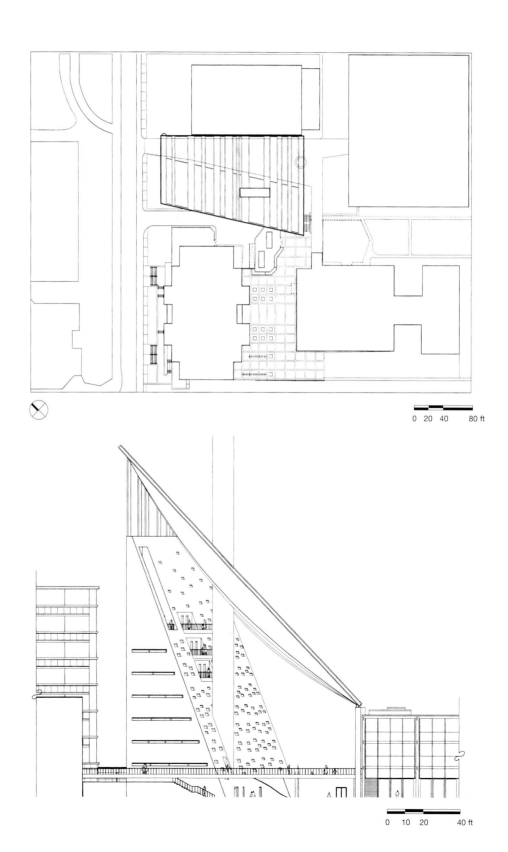

0 20 40   80 ft

0 10 20   40 ft

Silver Cities: China
for the Four Seasons Restaurant
1999

Designed by Philip Johnson for the company
FrancisFrancis!, these plates will be used by the
Four Seasons restaurant in New York City.
The gray-blue pattern features line-engraved
nineteenth-century partial plans of cities,
deliberately chosen to show the particular shape
of the city's form. The figure/ground of the street
lines and built blocks provides dense and
varied patterns to the place setting. The cities
represented are Genoa (225-millimeter bowl),
Milan (215-millimeter plate), Venice (coffee
cup), New York (coffee saucer), Brussels
(270-millimeter plate), Paris (304-millimeter
plate), Dublin (tea saucer), Marseilles (tea cup),
and Florence (206-millimeter bowl).

Children's Museum of Guadalajara

Guadalajara, Mexico

1999

The Guadalajara Children's Museum will be part of a larger cultural complex planned by the Mexican firm Omnilife. The museum sits on an island in a new man-made lake and will be accessed via a gatehouse and rope bridge. Four pavilions contain adaptable classroom spaces. These structures are plays on platonic solids: they distort the cube, sphere, cone, and pyramid. The theater is formed of clustered cubes; the classroom, of a coil; music study rooms, of truncated cones; the sculpture building, of a cluster of pyramids. Each of these buildings—experiments based on primary shapes—is part of an exploration of architecture for the children, too.

The buildings will be built from concrete, colored to resemble the native earth of the region. The interiors will instead be very brightly colored, to contrast with the outside brightness of the Mexican sun. The rest of the island will be open as a park.

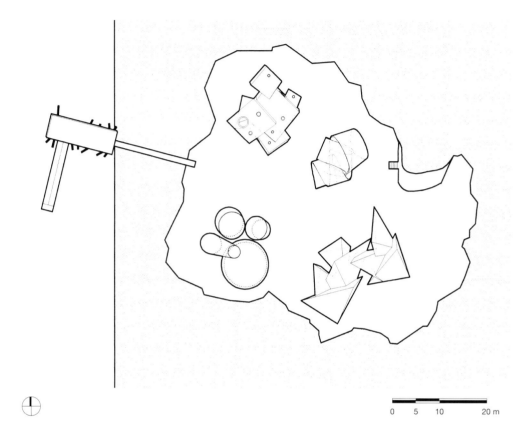

0   5   10   20 m

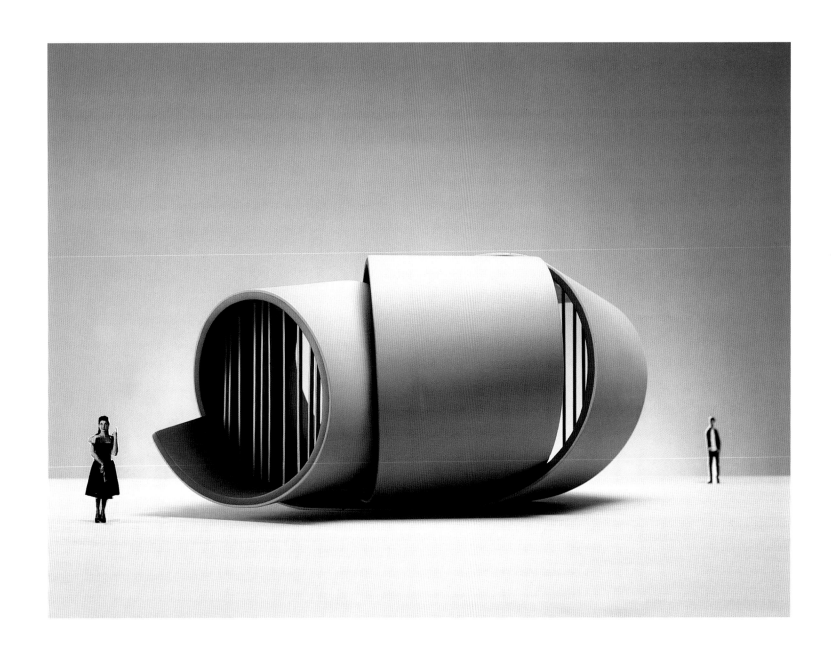

Guangzhou Opera House

Guangzhou, China
Design Competition
1999

The city of Guangzhou, on the Pearl River, is
developing a new city center and rehabilitating
its waterfront. In 1999 the city held a competition
for an opera house, intended to become
a symbol of cultural strength for the city.
The proposed scheme consists of a steel
structure 2,460 feet high—twice as tall as the
Eiffel Tower—and two opposing masses, one
housing the opera house, the other a museum.

The tower is of steel construction, restrained by
braces. Amoeba-shaped in plan, it is formed of
fifty vertical tubes. Diaphragm cables tie the
tubes together. Cables attached to each building
mass counterbalance the columnar structure and
eliminate the need to sustain large cantilevers at
the base.

Like the St. Louis Arch, the steel structure will
confer an air of spiritual and technical
magnificence to the city. Its top, reminiscent of a
spire, refers to the first architectural race to the
heavens, the Gothic church. The trio of
structures, with their cables, forms a gate on the
river, a marker for the new city center.

Philadelphia's Church of Our Savior

Philadelphia, Pennsylvania
1999

This cathedral is formed of two torqued ellipses. At the point of intersection, they make way for the main entry and, at the back, for a stretched window. The roof divides to receive a sheet of glass, which lights the altar below. The cathedral seats three thousand; it also accommodates a full orchestra and choir.

On the south facade, strips of stained glass puncture the thick walls, which will be covered in local stone. An adjoining cloister containing the church's administrative and educational facilities bounds a courtyard. Nearby, a twisted bell tower provides strong vertical contrast to the sweeping form of the cathedral.

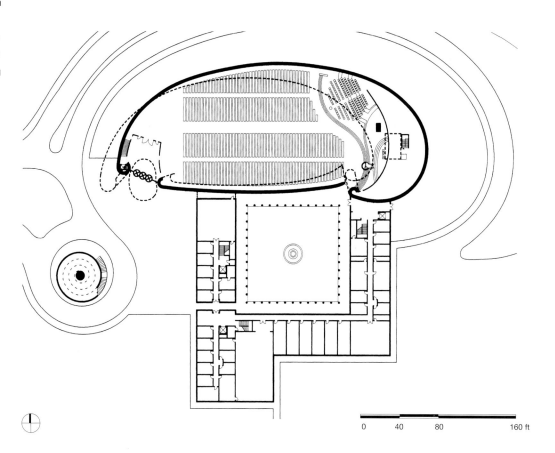

0   40   80   160 ft

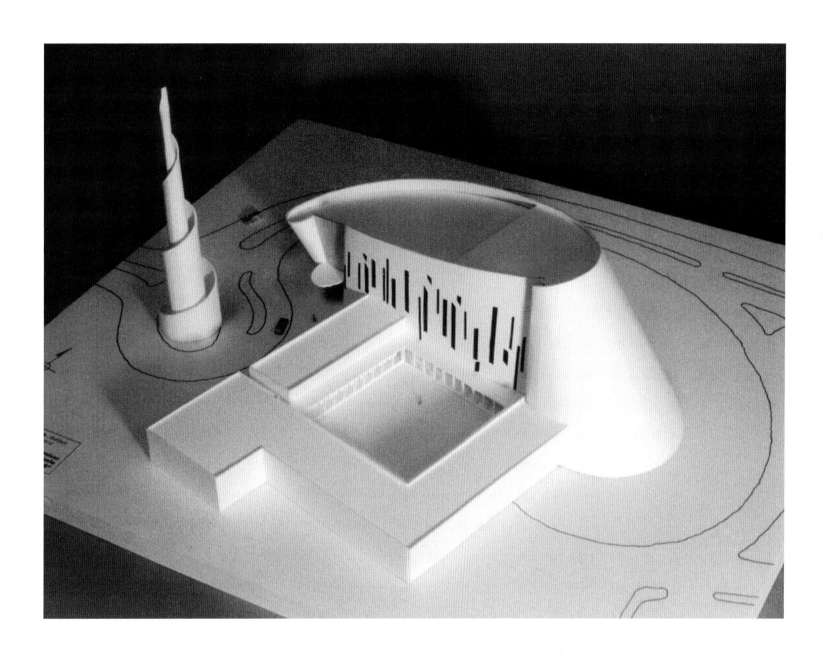

Venezuelan Consulate

New York, New York

1999

The Venezuelan Consulate is located on the East Side of Manhattan, within the shadow of the United Nations building. Developed by Alan Ritchie, the refitting and renovation included redesigning the interior floors, with the consulate on the first three floors and the ambassador's offices on the top three—both with new finishes—as well as inserting skylights, a rooftop garden, sculpture garden, gallery, and cafeteria. The renovation also involved recladding the building with a new curtain wall and garden facade. Partial floors were removed to create a triple-height entry at the lobby.

Rotterdam Tower

Rotterdam, Holland

1999

The firm's first major building in the Netherlands, this office tower, designed by Alan Ritchie, will occupy a narrow site on the Boompjes. While the structure takes its design cues from local buildings and conditions, the principal gesture—rotating the body of the tower at an angle—allows the offices optimum river views and sunlight; the curving facade to the north will offer sweeping views back to the city center. Designed for single tenant occupancy, floor plans will range from 785 to 925 square meters.

CBX Office Tower A at La Défense

Paris, France
Design Competition
1999

This is the first of two competition entries for an office tower. The site is a narrow sliver of undeveloped land at the perimeter of the La Défense business district near Paris. The first scheme was influenced by Mies van der Rohe's early glass tower schemes; its plan is shaped like a jagged lightning bolt. The points of the tower create a jagged, crenellated facade and contain winter gardens and conference rooms. A bridge pierces the glass tower at the pedestrian level.

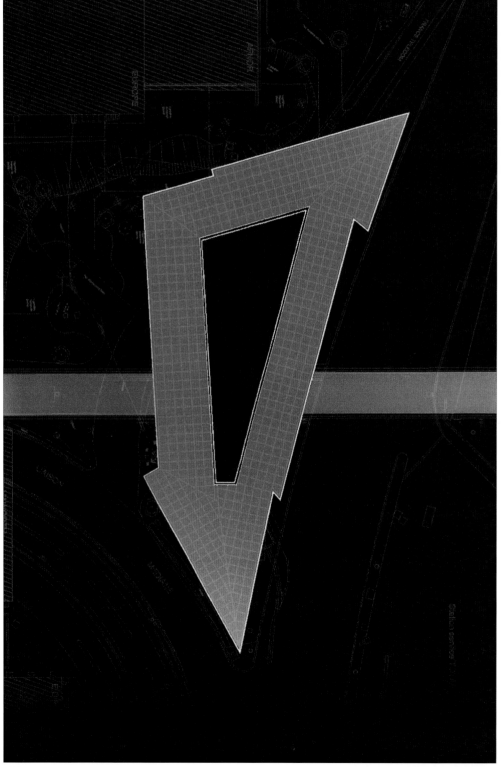

0   5   10 m

CBX Office Tower B at La Défense

Paris, France
Design Competition
1999

The second scheme for an office tower in
La Défense, near Paris, uses arcs in plan,
taking its cue from the narrow, curving streetfront, to present a more streamlined look than
the first scheme. Conceived by Alan Ritchie,
the curved tower stands in counterpoint to
the curve of the street below; the orthogonal
portion of its massing faces harmoniously
toward the rectangular towers of the
La Défense development.

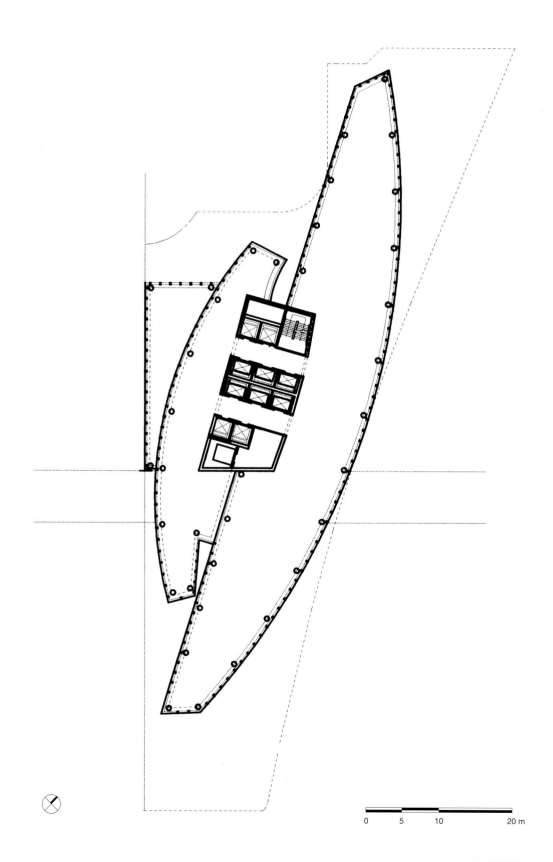

0   5   10   20 m

Pool House

Darien, Connecticut

1999

This design by Philip Johnson responded to a client's wish to install and enclose a pool in her backyard. The pool was to be accessible throughout the year, regardless of the season. The thirty-foot-high structure consists of a tall skeleton of curved I-beams clad in a glass skin, which boosts the temperature inside like a greenhouse. Cross-ventilation, through adjacent windows, provides passive cooling.

Inside, the hard lines of aluminum soften into shadows, repeating a rhythm of light and dark that moves with the sun. The height of the pool house, in visible contrast to the main house, and the interplay of light, shadow, and reflection suggest a clearing within tall trees, or a church. Bathed in light, the little house becomes a glass reliquary holding the pool within.

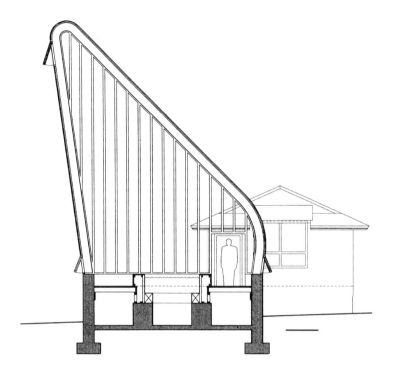

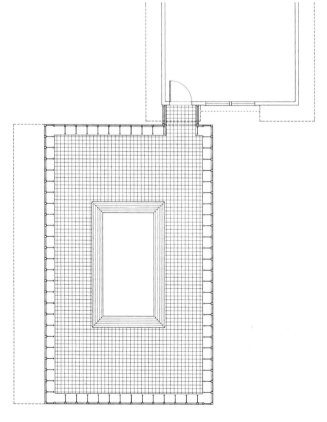

0   5   10 ft

The Oasis

Israel

1999

This vacation house and resort complex was designed for a desert site in Israel. Each building is formed from curving, free-form geometry similar to that of the Visitors' Pavilion at the Glass House. The individual structures are oriented internally; each typically contains a glass-walled atrium open to the sky. The pavilions intersect and cluster into groups that are arranged around a stone-paved courtyard and reflecting pool— hence the generating image of the project as a desert oasis.

A synagogue is shaped externally as a distorted, wave-washed stone cube and internally as a pure cubic space. Other structures on the grounds include tennis courts, pool, and carport.

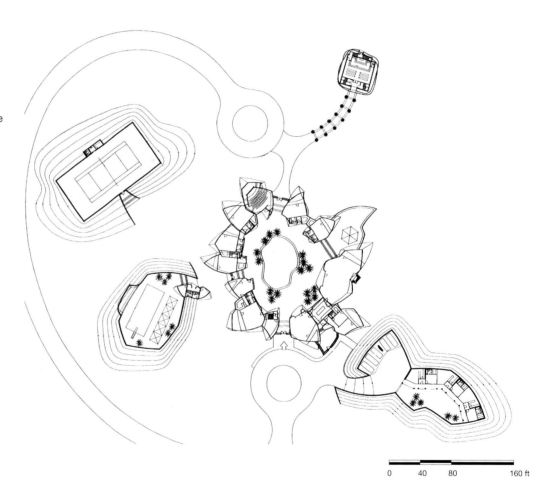

0   40   80   160 ft

Avenue des Morgines Office Complex

Geneva, Switzerland

1999

The challenge of the commission was to design a modern curtain-wall office building using massing identical to a recently demolished building on the same site and, in the process, unify the exterior design of the Avenue des Morgines Office Complex, an office park in Geneva. The curtain wall will contain an integrated shading system, a series of fabric sections that mechanically extend or retract for climate control. When extended, the brightly colored panels will add to the building's identity. The building will be clad in tinted glass and contain two separate lobbies, the larger one of which will house a café under a dramatic, sloped-glass skylight.

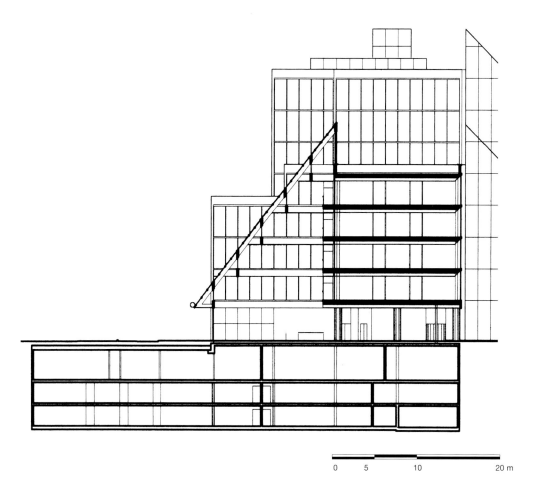

0   5   10   20 m

Domus Design Collection Furniture Showroom

New York, New York
1999

To strengthen its identity as a high-end furniture dealer, Domus Design Collection commissioned a new showroom in the shadow of the Empire State Building. The client was dissatisfied with traditional display windows, which limit access to the objects they contain. To solve this problem, the design integrates the window display into the space of the showroom, creating a series of vignettes, through which customers can walk, that are visible from the sidewalk. The presence of the shoppers examining furniture animates the window, creating a living frieze.

Two portals lead up into the light-soaked, glazed north side of the showroom. Interior walls, warped at different angles, form niches for furniture groupings. Visible from the street, they help to communicate the store's progressive identity to passersby.

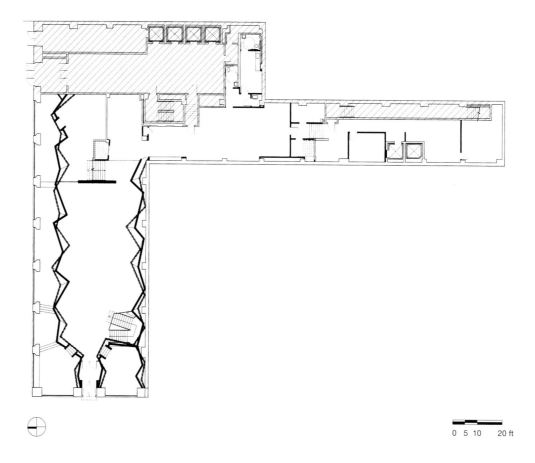

0 5 10   20 ft

Private Residence

Teaneck, New Jersey

2000

This residential design is Philip Johnson's Glass House turned inside out—a glass wall facing a courtyard. The massing of the house has its roots in Ledoux; the design features a main house and a guest house, which are connected by two glazed galleries, one lined with books and the other with closets.

The main building, to be used frequently for entertaining, consists of an entry foyer, double-height formal living and dining rooms, kitchen, master bedroom, and entertainment and exercise areas. The guest house is comprised of four individual units, each with a common area, two bedroom suites, and an interconnecting spiral stair. Cylindrical glass forms of varying sizes are used to enclose the stair towers of the guest rooms, extend the master bedroom, and create a reading rotunda off the north gallery.

Public facades are clad in stacked Vermont slate. The facades facing the courtyard are mullionless, water-white glass. All the roofs are copper with standing seams.

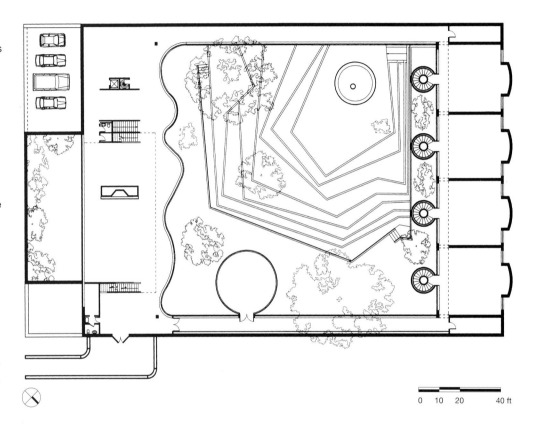

0   10   20   40 ft

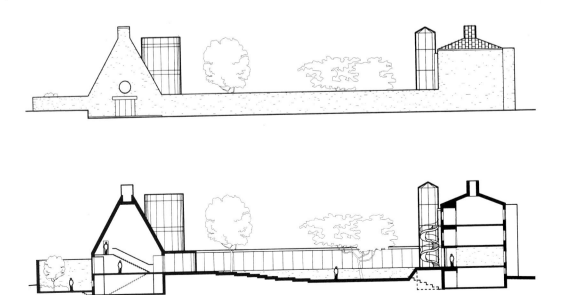

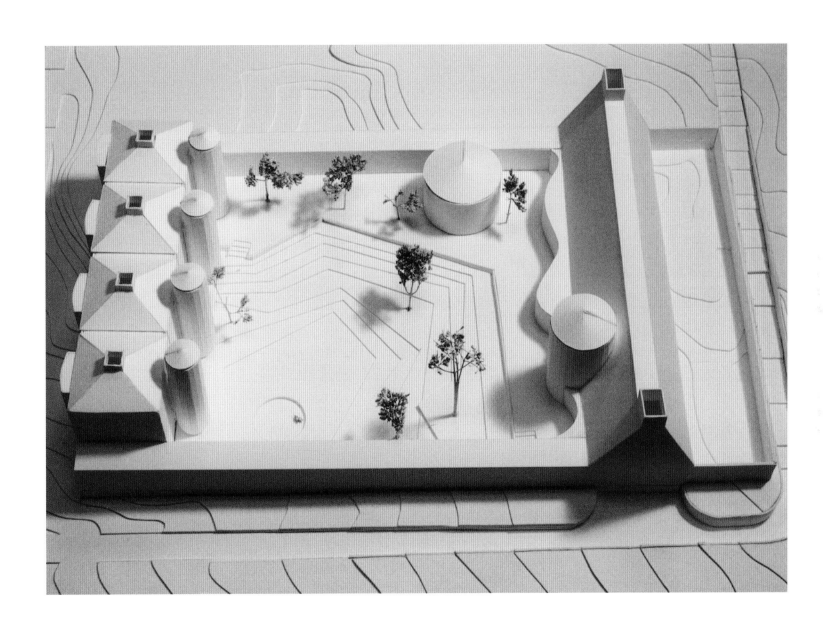

Chavasse Park Retail Center

Liverpool, England

2000

An urban development project on five and a half acres in the heart of Liverpool, the Chavasse Park Retail Center will link the city's main shopping area to the Albert Dock. The structure will house two department stores, other retail, theaters, and restaurants and will also create a pleasant winter garden in the city.

The roof, which provides the structure for the building, has its origins in the arcade. Sections of the roof spring down to the ground for support, while light penetrates between them. The interior space flows below the undulating surface of the roof. Landscaped gardens add to the open, parklike feeling of the space.

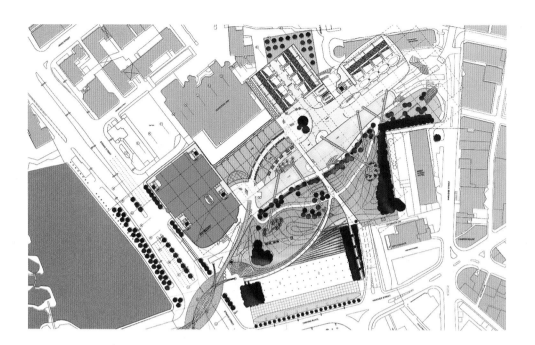

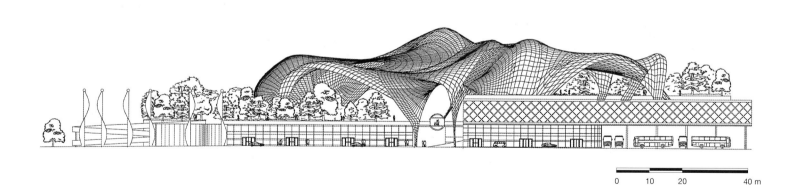

0   10   20   40 m

Vacation House on Providenciales

Turks and Caicos Islands

2000

This residence, to be built on a small island in the Turks and Caicos group, is composed of little pavilions grouped at three levels on a hill. The master suite is a cluster of linked pavilions, providing a self-sufficient hub. Guest quarters are scattered across the sloped landscape.

Though their scale varies, all sixteen pavilions have the same shape and proportions. Modeled on the Pantheon, each dome, a half sphere, rests on a cylinder. Each has an oculus measuring 20 percent of the sphere's diameter.

Stuccoed, with shuttered openings, the pavilions provide a profound sense of enclosure. They are designed as a contrast to the open landscape, a polarity intended to accentuate the experience of each.

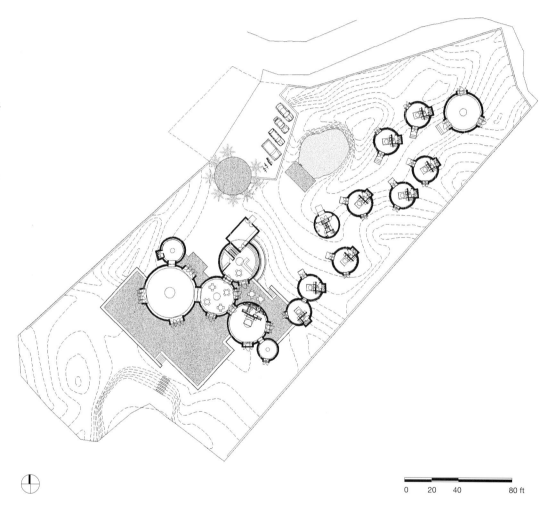

0   20   40   80 ft

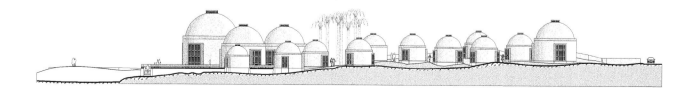

Apartments at 328 Spring Street

New York, New York

2000

A tower of lofts designed for residential use, the building is close to the entrance to the Holland Tunnel, in a neighborhood of brick warehouses and loft buildings that have been converted by artists to residences and studios. A sculpture of twisted steel by John Chamberlain was the initial inspiration for the massing of the twenty-seven-story building. To create the effect of a bundled collage of Tribeca loft structures, the tower will be constructed from a rich palette of differently colored bricks with varied window shapes, sizes, and ornamental details.

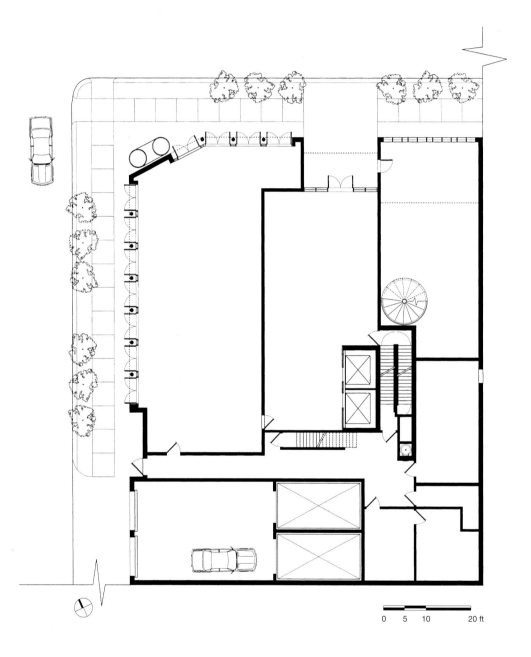

0   5   10   20 ft

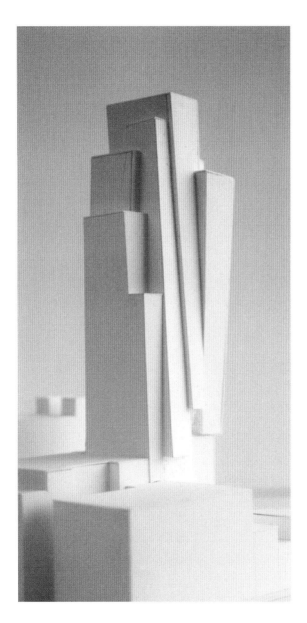
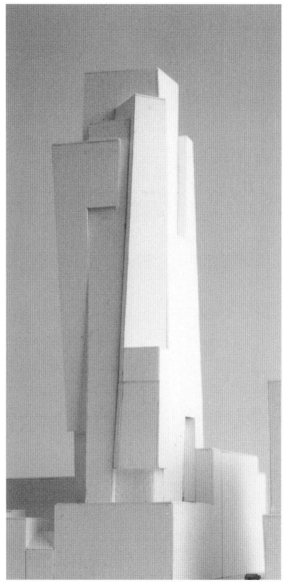

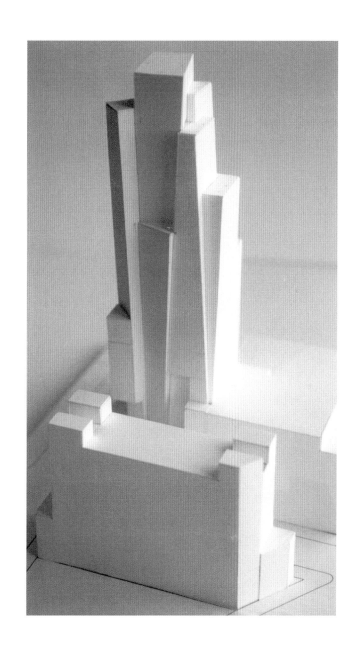

A.I.G. Headquarters Building

Hong Kong, China
Design Competition
2000

Six architectural firms participated in a design
competition for A.I.G.'s new headquarters
building in Hong Kong. The significant location
and proximity to the Hong Kong waterfront offer
A.I.G. a unique opportunity to develop an office
building that will impact the already highly
recognizable Hong Kong skyline.

Alan Ritchie's inspiration for the design was
drawn from the many ships that constantly criss-
cross Victoria Harbor, which gracefully unfolds
beyond city hall to the north, and also the number
eight, a Chinese character that is said to bring
fortune and good will. While many of the existing
buildings face the water in an axial relationship,
this design was oriented on the site at an angle
of forty-five degrees to take full advantage of the
views of the harbor and to open the public street
level toward Chater Gardens. This provides both
a visual and physical connection between
Connaught Road and the gardens.

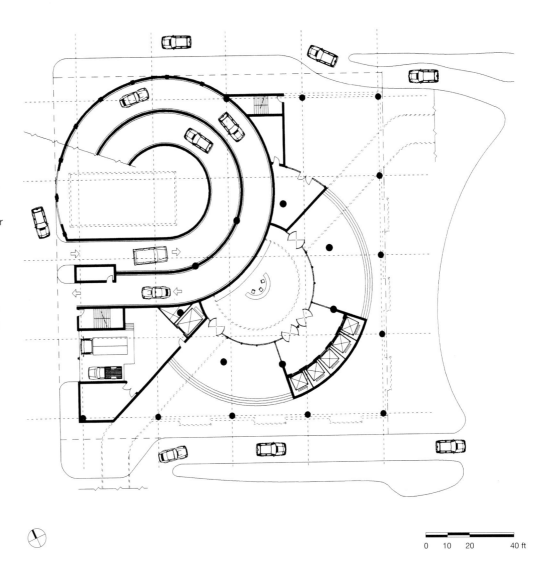

0   10   20   40 ft

Employee List

Philip Johnson/Alan Ritchie Architects
thanks the following individuals,
whose talents and dedication have
generously contributed to the success
of these projects and to our office:

Principals
Alan Ritchie
Philip Johnson

Former Principals
Elizabeth Murrell
David Fiore

Senior Associate
John Manley

Yasin Abdulla
Doug Alligood
Christian Bjone
Oreste Bosko
Karin Bruckner
Nick Buccalo
Tatiana Cabal
Ignatius Caramia
Linda Casper
Cristina Castro
Gigi Fernandez
B. Pietro Filardo
Suzanne Gehlert
Franca Giammarino
Angus Goble
Barry Gordon
Deborah Greene
David Harrison
Barbara Hartman
Rolf Hedlund
Adam Hird
Rosa Hurtado
Peter Johantgen
Gordon Kipping
Maureen Knorr
Ling Li
Ken Lin
Aaron McDonald
Hiroshi Nakamura
Don Porter
Paul Preissner
Ana Sanchez
Carola Sapper
Benjamin Schaeffer
Richard Schneider
Duane Schrempp
Beverly Skelton
Richard Tayson
Dennis Wedlick
Winston Williams
Amanda Wolf
Barbara Wolfe

Project Credits

St. Basil Chapel at the University of St. Thomas
Houston, Texas
1991
Associate Architect: Merriman Holt Architects
Structural Engineer: Cagley, Conti & Jumper
Mechanical/Electrical Engineering: CHP & Associates
Lighting Consultant: Claude R. Engle
Photographs: Richard Payne

Millennia Walk in Pontiac Marina
Singapore
1992
Associate Architect: DP Architects PGE
Structural Engineer: Leslie E. Robertson
Mechanical/Electrical Engineering: Cosentini & Associates
Lighting Consultant: Claude R. Engle
Photographs: Alan Ritchie

American Business Center at Checkpoint Charlie
Berlin, Germany
1992
Associate Architect: Pysall, Stahrenberg & Partners
Structural Engineer: Leonhardt, Andra und Partner
Mechanical/Electrical Engineering: Flack and Kurtz Consulting Engineers
Photographs: Richard Payne

Berlin Fantasy
Berlin, Germany
1992
Model: Joe Santeramo
Photographs: Robert Walker

Greater Shanghai Shopping Center
Shanghai, China
Design Competition
1993
Rendering: 3D/The Drawing Studio

Borden Hall, Manhattan School of Music
New York, New York
1993
Photographs: Michael Rogol

Visitor's Pavilion (Da Monsta), Glass House
New Canaan, Connecticut
1993
Structural Engineer: Ysrael Seinuk P.C.
Lighting Consultant: Claude R. Engle
Photographs: Michael Moran (exterior); Norman McGrath (interior)

Berlin Glockenturm
Berlin, Germany
1994
Model: Joe Santeramo
Photographs: Robert Walker

Riverside South Residential Towers
New York, New York
1994
Associate Architect: CK Architects
Structural Engineer: Cantor Seinuk Group, Inc.
Mechanical/Electrical Engineering: I. M. Robbins
Landscape Architect: Thomas Balsley Associates
Rendering: Tesla
Photographs: Richard Payne

National Museum of Korea
Seoul, Korea
Design Competition
1994
Associate Architect: Anderson & Oh, Inc.
Model: Richard Tenguerian
Photographs: Michael Rogol

Sugar Foods Corporate Offices
New York, New York
1994
Mechanical/Electrical Engineering: Motola Rini Engineers, P.C.
Photographs: Michael Rogol

New Art Center at Century Center
South Bend, Indiana
1995
Associate Architect: Matthews Purucker Anella, Inc.
Structural Engineer: Gregory M. Tkachyk, P.E.
Mechanical/Electrical Engineering: M & E Design Services
Lighting Consultant: M & E Design Services

Cathedral of Hope

Dallas, Texas

1995

Structural Engineer: Leslie E. Robertson Associates

Mechanical/Electrical Engineering: Cosentini Associates

Lighting Consultant: Claude R. Engle

Model: Richard Tenguerian

Photographs: Michael Rogol, Bates Photography

Celebration Town Hall

Celebration, Florida

1995

Associate Architect: HKS, Inc.

Structural Engineer: HKS Structural

Mechanical/Electrical Engineering: Blum Consulting Engineers

Photographs: William Taylor

Trump International Hotel and Tower

New York, New York

1995

Associate Architect: CK Architects

Structural Engineer: Cantor Seinuk Group, Inc.

Mechanical/Electrical Engineering: I. M. Robbins

Lighting Consultant: Claude R. Engle

Landscape Architect: Thomas Balsley Associates

Rendering: Richard C. Baehr

Photographs: Richard Payne

Ville de Tremblay

Paris, France

1995

Associate Architect: M. F. France, Massimiliano Fuksas

***Turning Point* at Case Western Reserve University**

Cleveland, Ohio

1996

Fabricator: Merrifield-Roberts, Inc.

Structural Engineer: C. A. Pretzer Associates, Inc.

Lighting Consultant: Claude R. Engle

Photographs: Richard Payne

***TimeSculpture* at Lincoln Center**

New York, New York

1996

Fabricator: Merrifield-Roberts, Inc.

Structural Engineer: C. A. Pretzer Associates, Inc.

Mechanical/Electrical Engineering: Motola Rini Engineers, P.C.

Graphic Design Consultant: 2x4

Rendering: Michael Rock

Photographs: Robert Walker

McKinley Center Master Plan

Manila, Philippines

1996

Associate Architect: Recio + Casas

Rendering: 3D/The Drawing Studio

Abu Dhabi Investment Authority Headquarters

Abu Dhabi, U.A.E.

Design Competition

1996

Model: Gene Cevini

Photographs: Robert Walker

Amon Carter Museum Expansion

Fort Worth, Texas

1997

Associate Architect: Carter & Burgess

Structural Engineer: Datum Engineering

Mechanical/Electrical Engineering: Blum Consulting Engineers

Lighting Consultant: Gordon Hansen

Landscape Architect: Carter & Burgess

Model: Richard Tenguerian

Photographs: Amon Carter Museum; Richard Payne, 97

Times Square Site 3

New York, New York

1997

Structural Engineer: DeSimone Chaplin & Dobryn

Lighting Consultant: Fernando Vasquez and Sussman/Preza Graphics

Rendering: Kupiec & Koutsomitiz

Model: Richard Tenguerian

Photographs: Robert Walker

Times Square Site 4
New York, New York
1997
Structural Engineer: DeSimone Chaplin & Dobryn
Lighting Consultant: Fernando Vasquez and Sussman/Preza Graphics
Rendering: Fernando Vasquex
Model: Richard Tenguerian
Photographs: Robert Walker

Turning Point Park at Case Western Reserve University
Cleveland, Ohio
1998
Fabricator: Merrifield Roberts, Inc.
Structural Engineer: C. A. Pretzer Associates, Inc.
Photographs: Richard Payne

Chrysler Center East Tower Renovation and Expansion
New York, New York
1998
Associate Architect: Adamson Associates
Structural Engineer: Severud Associates
Mechanical/Electrical Engineering: Syska & Hennessy, Inc.
Lighting Consultant: Claude R. Engle
Photographs: Richard Payne

333 Westchester Avenue
White Plains, New York
1998
Associate Architect: Design Collaborative
Fabricator: Merrifield-Roberts, Inc.
Structural Engineer: Thornton-Tomasetti
Mechanical/Electrical Engineering: Edwards and Zuck
Lighting Consultant: Claude R. Engle
Landscape Architect: Thomas Balsley Associates
Rendering: Pixel by Pixel

First Union Plaza
Boca Raton, Florida
1998
Associate Architect: Retzsch Lanao Caycedo Architects
Photographs: Richard Payne

Ski House
Telluride, Colorado
1998
Model: Philip Johnson/Alan Ritchie Architects
Photographs: Robert Walker

Chain Link Garden Pavilion
North Salem, New York
1999
Fabricator: Merrifield-Roberts, Inc.
Structural Engineer: C. A. Pretzer Associates, Inc.
Photographs: Paul Warchol

Texas A&M School of Architecture
College Station, Texas
1999
Model: Philip Johnson/Alan Ritchie Architects
Photographs: Roy J. Wright

Silver Cities: China for the Four Seasons Restaurant
1999
Photographs: Philip Johnson/Alan Ritchie Architects

Children's Museum of Guadalajara
Guadalajara, Mexico
1999
Model: Richard Tenguerian
Photographs: Robert Walker

Guangzhou Opera House
Guangzhou, China
Design Competition
1999
Structural Engineer: Cecil Balmond/Ove Arup Associates
Model: Richard Tenguerian
Photographs: Robert Walker

Philadelphia's Church of Our Savior
Philadelphia, Pennsylvania
1999
Model: Philip Johnson/Alan Ritchie Architects
Photographs: Robert Walker

Venezuelan Consulate
New York, New York
1999
Rendering: Visual Information, Inc.

Rotterdam Tower
Rotterdam, Holland
1999
Associate Architect: Brouwer Steketee Architecten
Structural Engineer: D3BN Den Haag
Mechanical/Electrical Engineering: Hori raadgevend Ingenieursbureau b.v.
Rendering: Brouwer Steketee Architecten

CBX Office Tower A at La Défense
Paris, France
Design Competition
1999
Structural Engineer: Cantor Seinuk Group, Inc.
Rendering: Adamson Associates
Model: Philip Johnson/Alan Ritchie Architects
Photographs: Robert Walker

CBX Office Tower B at La Défense
Paris, France
Design Competition
1999
Structural Engineer: Cantor Seinuk Group, Inc.
Model: Philip Johnson/Alan Ritchie Architects
Photographs: Robert Walker

Pool House
Darien, Connecticut
1999
Model: Philip Johnson/Alan Ritchie Architects
Photographs: Robert Walker

The Oasis
Israel
1999
Model: Richard Tenguerian
Photographs: Philip Johnson/Alan Ritchie Architects

Avenue des Morgines Office Complex
Geneva, Switzerland
1999
Associate Architect: Favre Guth & Architectes Associés, S.A.
Rendering: Sven Johnson

Domus Design Collection Furniture Showroom
New York, New York
1999
Structural Engineer: HAGE Engineering
Mechanical/Electrical Engineering: Bladykas Engineering, P.C.
Lighting Consultant: Claude R. Engle
Model: Philip Johnson/Alan Ritchie Architects
Photographs: Paul Warchol

Private Residence
Teaneck, New Jersey
2000
Model: Philip Johnson/Alan Ritchie Architects
Photographs: Philip Johnson/Alan Ritchie Architects

Chavasse Park Retail Center
Liverpool, England
2000
Associate Architect: Studio BAAD
Structural Engineer: Cecil Balmond/Ove Arup Associates
Rendering: Studio BAAD

Vacation House on Providenciales
Turks and Caicos Islands
2000
Associate Architect: Rothermel Cook Associates
Model: Philip Johnson/Alan Ritchie Architects

Apartments at 328 Spring Street
New York, New York
2000
Associate Architect: Thomas O'Hara Architect P.L.L.C.
Mechanical/Electrical Engineering: Joseph R. Loring & Associates, Inc.
Model: Philip Johnson/Alan Ritchie Architects
Photographs: Philip Johnson/Alan Ritchie Architects

A.I.G. Headquarters Building

Hong Kong, China

Design Competition

2000

Structural Engineer: Leslie E. Robertson

Mechanical/Electrical Engineering: Cosentini & Associates

Rendering: Philip Johnson/Alan Ritchie Architects

Model: Philip Johnson/Alan Ritchie Architects

Photographs: Philip Johnson/Alan Ritchie Architects

Biographies

Born and trained in England, Alan Ritchie has worked side by side with Philip Johnson for more than twenty-five years. In 1994 they formed the firm Philip Johnson/Alan Ritchie Architects, P.C., where Ritchie is the president. In their collaborations, Ritchie takes Johnson's initial concepts, develops the designs, and oversees the realization of the buildings. In addition, Ritchie expresses his own creative talents, designing many of the firm's projects. Philip Johnson/Alan Ritchie Architects, P.C., has developed a practice known worldwide for large- and small-scale designs that consistently challenge traditional architectural boundaries and continually reshape buildings into new works of architectural and sculptural form.

Philip Johnson, who turned ninety-five in 2001, is still actively involved with many of the projects designed by Philip Johnson/Alan Ritchie Architects, P.C. A towering eminence in his field, he continues to exercise his remarkable influence on the shaping of contemporary architecture. Johnson brings to the firm a master's understanding of the limits and possibilities of his craft as well as a creativity that informs the firm's growing practice.

DATE DUE

GAYLORD | | | PRINTED IN U.S.A.